Every Child Can Learn

Every Child Can Learn

Using Learning Tools and play to help children with developmental delay

Katrin Stroh, Thelma Robinson and Alan Proctor

Illustrated by Jane Dickson

Los Angeles • London • New Delhi • Singapore

SAGE Publications Ltd
1 Oliver's Yard
55 City Road
London EC1Y 1SP

SAGE Publications Inc.
2455 Teller Road
Thousand Oaks, California 91320

SAGE Publications India Pvt Ltd
B 1/I 1 Mohan Cooperative Industrial Area
Mathura Road
New Delhi 110 044

SAGE Publications Asia-Pacific Pte Ltd
33 Pekin Street #02-01
Far East Square
Singapore 048763

Library of Congress Control Number: 2007940171

British Library Cataloguing in Publication Data

A catalogue record for this book is available from the British Library

ISBN 978-1-4129-4794-7
ISBN 978-1-4129-4795-4 (pbk)

Typeset by C&M Digitals (P) Ltd, Chennai, India
Printed and bound by CPI Group (UK) Ltd, Croydon, CR0 4YY
Printed on paper from sustainable resources

We would like to dedicate this book to the many children and families who have shared their pain and their joy and from whom we have learned so much.

COMMENTS ABOUT FUNCTIONAL LEARNING

'I never considered just how important curiosity is in learning. The ability to be curious – that is what all children must be given.'

Father, Essex

'I am now aware of the many possibilities for learning situations at home that can be devised from simple principles.'

Mother, Essex

'We obviously have a long way to go with Matthew, but I feel that Functional Learning can help him reach his full potential and no one else has offered him that.'

Mother, Yorkshire

'I'm needed here!'

4-year-old boy after a Functional Learning session with Geoffrey Waldon

'Why do I find it so easy now [to learn] when I used to find it so difficult?'

8-year-old boy working with Functional Learning

COMMENTS ABOUT THE VIDEO
LEARNING AND COMMUNICATION

'I have nothing but praise for your video, it was so wonderfully clear and simple. Anyone would be able to understand it and it seems a perfect way to promote your ideas.'

Robin Skynner, Family therapist

'The emphasis is on learning in the broadest sense – therapists and others will be immediately struck by the [quiet] learning environment … often found when very young children play intently by themselves'

Professor David Crystal

'Your approach [Functional Learning] ought to be part of the repertoire of any therapist when working with children with delayed development.'

Dr John Richer, Clinical Psychologist

'The theoretical framework and the practical guidance for implementation will offer parents and professionals much to emulate … it makes a valuable contribution to our understanding of how young children learn … using detailed observations of what children do in their spontaneous play.'

Dorothy Rouse, National Children's Bureau

Contents

Contents of CD

Acknowledgements

We would like to express our gratitude to the late Dr Geoffrey Waldon, neurologist and pioneering educator, who we first met in 1976. He introduced us to his ideas on the development of play, learning and the Learning Tools in the young child. His generosity in sharing his knowledge helped to shape our own practice. Functional Learning, our integrative approach, incorporates Waldon's basic learning ideas and techniques. Over the years, we have extended and developed these ideas and techniques, standardizing and simplifying them, informed by our own work with children and families.

The gestation of this book has taken many years. We have been helped, guided, supported and encouraged by many friends and colleagues. Katrin Stroh would like to thank the following: the late Nancy Raphael and her Educational Trust which sponsored the original video, *Learning and Communication*; Annette Lawson and The Judith Trust who gave generous funding for the book illustrations; Caroline Raphael who also contributed to the illustrations; enthusiastic colleagues from Slovenia who have been working with Functional Learning for 12 years, and particularly Ana Filipic Dolnicar, Barbara Somen, Nena Vovk and Slavica Lencek; Mijana Durovic and Save the Children Fund which sponsored Functional Learning workshops in Montenegro; Ilse Dittrich, colleague and close friend for over 30 years, who supported the introduction of Functional Learning to the Bonhoeffer House day centre in Hanover, Germany; Margie Wagner of Child Development Media, Inc. in California, who has always been enthusiastic about introducing Functional Learning resources to the USA. There have been thoughtful and stimulating discussions with many people over the years and particularly: Professor Lionel Hersov and Zoe Hersov who have always given encouragement; Stephen Scott MD; Richard Brooks who has been positive and supportive; Anita Hughes; Jane Blatt and Toby Stroh; Sophie Laws; Sophie Levitt; Elaine Leader from Teen Line USA; Howard Sharron; Peter Hobson; and Professor Mike Rutter, a friend and constant supporter.

We are extremely grateful to Mary Proctor whose skill and creativity in preparing the CD material have been absolutely invaluable.

To Marianne Lagrange whose belief, trust and guidance enabled this book to be published, our thanks are boundless. Thank you to Matthew Waters for practical advice and suggestions during the preparation of the manuscript and CD, and to Bob McCormick who generously shared his knowledge which set us on the right path at the beginning.

Finally, this work would not have been possible without the insight and experience of George Stroh, whose unique blend of applied psychodynamics and humanity laid the foundation for Functional Learning.

CASE STUDIES

We would like to thank the parents of Tony (not his real name), his school, and support teacher for giving their permission to include the information in Chapter 18. The other descriptions of children and families included in this book are composite examples based on children and families seen in our clinical practice, apart from Eleanor, Helen and Christopher who appear in the video on the CD and Jonathan (not his real name) who was the subject of a previous journal article (Stroh and Robinson, 1991).

About the Authors

The authors all worked in the 1970s at High Wick Hospital, a specialist children's unit with an international reputation for its research and innovative treatment programmes, where they were involved in the development of Functional Learning as an integrated therapeutic approach.

Katrin Stroh is a Speech and Language Therapist, Social Worker and Developmental Therapist with over 40 years experience. Since 1982 she has worked in her own practice in London specializing in Functional Learning programmes for young children with developmental delay and their families, also running training workshops in the UK and in Europe, the United States and Australia.

Thelma Robinson is a Clinical Psychologist, Montessori teacher and Developmental Therapist. She has experience of many different settings including child psychiatry and a speech and language centre. In 1986 she joined Katrin Stroh in her London practice, working with children and parents, and collaborating with publishing papers, producing a video and running workshops to introduce Functional Learning.

Alan Proctor is a teacher, qualified to work with emotionally disturbed children, as well as a Counsellor and Developmental Therapist. He has over 30 years experience working with children and families, which gave rise to teaching in Further Education and running workshops in the UK and abroad. His work with adults mainly deals with childhood abuse and bereavement.

Thank goodness there is now a clear and practical guide to this groundbreaking technique. The unique teaching approach described in this book helps children – even those with severe learning difficulties – to learn how to be ready to learn, spontaneously, from all their daily experiences. It is so well presented and explained here that I'm determined to recommend it to all the professionals and parents I meet. The originality of the approach is startling and the results fascinating both for students and teachers. This is the ultimate way to teach open-ended thinking and problem-solving skills to children whose emotional and developmental difficulties make it hard for them to learn.

Richard Brooks, Advanced Practitioner
Oxfordshire Service for Autism

Glossary

This glossary is intended as a guide to the most frequently used terms referred to in the book.

A-social or non-social
Describes the learning conditions of the Functional Learning sessions, similar to those experienced by the young child when they are playing and learning by themselves. The adult is there in the background to make sure the child feels safe and secure, but there is little or no social interaction between them at this time. There are no social rewards – the satisfaction comes from the activity itself.

Continuant behaviour
A term used by Geoffrey Waldon (1980) to refer to the way young children move objects continuously from one place to another, gaining experience about the qualities of objects – appearance, size, shape, weight, texture and position in space.

Cross-cultural
The exploratory play and learning of the young child, common to all cultures. Functional Learning, based on this early activity, can easily be adapted to suit different cultural environments.

Developmental delay
A general term to refer to children whose development has not kept pace with the norm. It looks at the child from a more holistic developmental perspective in preference to using specific diagnostic labels.

Functional Learning
An integrated therapeutic approach based on the growth and development of the normal child. The central focus is the development of Learning Tools, but it also recognizes the important connection between emotions and learning.

Guiding hand
Used in the Functional Learning sessions, when the adult guides the child's hands by holding their hands over the child's hands to help them with the activities.

Innate
Present from birth. Children have an innate capacity for play which takes place without instruction.

Integrated therapeutic approach
A comprehensive approach that involves all aspects of the child's development – learning, language and communication, and emotional growth. It tries to meet the needs of each child and family by crossing professional boundaries and working collaboratively with parents and carers.

Learning Tools
What Geoffrey Waldon (1980) referred to as the learning-how-to-learn tools, mental tools which all children use to learn about the world around them:

Placing – picking things up and putting them down

Piling – moving a variety of objects in a continuous way to make a pile or heap

Banging – holding an object, bringing it into contact with another object or surface

Pairing – putting together two objects or images that are the same

Matching – comparing or contrasting one object or image with another

Sorting – recognizing that objects or images can be grouped together in sets

Sequencing – arranging things one following another

Brick Building – placing bricks in different positions in relation to one another

Pointing finger
The pointing gesture that infants develop during the last part of the first year. It is one of the earliest pre-verbal communications. The pointing finger is used extensively in many of the learning activities.

Potential
The capacity for growth and development. Every child has the potential for learning through the development of Learning Tools.

Secondary defensive behaviour
Responses used by the developmentally delayed child to overcome anxiety, fear and displeasure. They are ways of keeping to the familiar and avoiding change which means they interfere with normal learning. They can include physical

withdrawal, noisy protest, throwing and the more extreme headbanging, rocking, or spinning objects.

Seeding
Placing one or more objects in a container or cards on a board as a model during sorting activities, minimizing the need for verbal instructions and enabling the child to work out for themselves what to do.

Separating
A way of sorting a pile or container of objects by choosing from the same set each time, rather than spontaneously picking up objects at random.

Social learning
Learning influenced by other people, which may involve rewards or praise, reflecting the culture the child lives in and the kind of skills that are important in that culture.

Introduction

This book is about enabling children with developmental delay to achieve their potential. It is based on our own clinical practice. Our unique approach is Functional Learning where the central focus is on helping children learn, but the child's feelings and relationships are always taken into account and we work within the family. For 30 years we have been working with children of all ages with learning difficulties, in a variety of different settings and with many different diagnoses. We now want to share with others the enthusiasm, pleasure and success that we have experienced. We have written this book for anyone working with or caring for children with developmental delay, those running training courses for early years workers, teacher training and child development courses, as well as parents.

We have included some historical background to our own work and a theoretical context, and we have highlighted similarities and differences with other approaches in this field. But our main focus is always on the practical work, techniques and activities we have used to enable children to develop their learning, and to be able to play and communicate. It is our firm belief that every child can learn. We have always worked within a positive framework. So often parents and carers have focused on what their child cannot do, and they experience intense relief and a feeling of hope when they understand that their child has a potential for learning.

Our Functional Learning approach, based on the play and learning of a normal young child, is cross-cultural. It can easily be adapted by practitioners anywhere who have this common background of knowledge of normal development. They will find that they can add these techniques to their own working practices with immediate positive results. A centre in Slovenia has adopted the Functional Learning approach and one of the special needs teachers has described the impact this has had on their work. Before they discovered Functional Learning, they experienced certain constraints and a sense of helplessness about their lack of progress with children who had severe developmental difficulties. They felt that the children were not responding to the procedures and methods they were using. The Functional Learning programme showed them clearly how to work in a creative and flexible way within the child's current developmental level.

We want to make the work as accessible as possible to those who are interested in this method of helping children learn. With this in mind, we have described the learning materials and activities in considerable detail, with illustrations to clarify the text. Although some commercially available toys and equipment can be used, for the most part the materials are common everyday objects that can be collected by anyone, at little expense. Many of the activities use sets of cards, and these can be made by practitioners and parents. Included with the book is a CD, with a video of children at work, many ideas for materials that can be used in the learning activities, and printable material for making cards and worksheets. A CD icon is used throughout the book wherever there is a reference to the CD.

ABOUT THE BOOK

The book is a practical manual organized into five integrated sections. Section I introduces the historical background to Functional Learning, makes links with normal play and the development of learning based on the concept of Learning Tools, and describes how to set up Functional Learning sessions based on an integral process of assessment and treatment.

Sections II and III explain in detail how to facilitate individual Learning Tools and how the use of Learning Tools encourages independent learning.

Section IV is concerned with the development of language and communication, parent/family support and feeding as a therapeutic tool.

Section V describes Functional Learning in different settings, including mainstream education, and looks at the cross-cultural dimension, ending with a suggested workshop programme to introduce Functional Learning.

SECTION I

FUNCTIONAL LEARNING THEORY AND PRACTICE

This section sets the scene and provides the context for the rest of the book. The ideas on normal play and learning may sound familiar but the concept of Learning Tools is a different way of looking at children's learning. It will become clear that Functional Learning, the therapeutic approach based on these new ideas, has proved to be successful cross-culturally in helping children with developmental delay.

1

Historical Background

CONTENTS

♦ The need

♦ A place to meet the need

♦ Developing ideas

♦ Putting theory into practice

♦ Functional Learning

1.1 THE NEED

'You have made the impossible possible.' These were the words of Anna Freud when she visited High Wick, a unique, pioneering residential children's centre (Stroh, 1986). The need for the centre to help some of the most puzzling children had been recognized years earlier. A report by Ruth Thomas (1964), coordinator for the work at High Wick Hospital, explained the problem that the Hampstead Child Therapy Clinic hoped the centre would deal with. It referred to 'borderline children' who 'seem to lack understanding in so many areas of thought and perception as to give a bizarre impression ... they appear unable to play except in strange repetitive fashions'. The report continues, 'this is a field where [we are] considerably at a loss to meet the challenge to our understanding', indicating that there was a great need for a unit to support these children and their families. High Wick eventually met this need, caring for a wide range of children we would now describe as developmentally delayed. Parents were not necessarily given a label for their child but an indication of what the hospital could do for the child and the family.

1.2 A PLACE TO MEET THE NEED

High Wick was a small, psychodynamically-oriented hospital originally set up in 1954, caring for 18 children aged between three and 12 years with learning, language and emotional problems. It was part of the National Health Service and Dr George Stroh was Consultant Psychiatrist-in-charge from 1958 until his death in 1979. The school, which was an integral part of the unit, came under the Local Education Authority. The large house near St Albans in Hertfordshire, which was High Wick Hospital, was described by Dr Stroh as 'child friendly' with its corners and staircases. The children were at the centre of this unit in its physical structure and its thinking. Staff accommodation for the childcare workers was in a separate house across the road, Highfield Hall, which included special resources for research projects. High Wick became known internationally as a centre for the care of, and research into, understanding these difficult children who were seen as a challenge.

1.3 DEVELOPING IDEAS

CHILD DEVELOPMENT

Ruth Thomas also referred to the staff training carried out by Dr Max Goldblatt (1964), a medical analyst who visited the unit once a week, and who said in his own report, 'The subject of the lecture-seminars has been "Normal Child Development"'. Knowledge of normal child development was to become increasingly important and eventually led to the videoing of a child at regular intervals from birth to three years. Such in-depth child observation arose in part from Dr Stroh commenting that, in order to help the range of children at High Wick, it was important to know how children learn.

QUIET ENVIRONMENT AND SECONDARY DEFENCE BEHAVIOUR

The children at High Wick exhibited difficult behaviour and did not have a normal pattern of learning. A study was set up to observe and describe the reactions of two autistic children in an environment where there was little to disturb or confuse them. A paper on the study (Stroh and Buick, 1970) concludes, 'These findings seem to support our hypothesis that reduction of sensory input will lead to more appropriate use of sensory modalities'. These children, who used to screw up their eyes so they did not look or see, and put their hands over their ears so they did not hear, were now looking, hearing and even playing peek-a-boo. They had begun to move towards a more normal response pattern which would give the potential for more normal learning to take place. One of the important ideas that came out of this early work was the concept of secondary defence behaviours to describe behaviour such as the avoidance of looking or hearing, screaming, running away, which children used to protect themselves from underlying fears and anxieties.

FEEDING AND THE TAKING-IN EXPERIENCE

The experience of the children in the quiet environment set the scene for additional work with children and feeding. The setting was a one-to-one situation in a quiet environment away from the general hustle and bustle of daily life and mealtimes of the unit. The underlying assumption of this therapeutic programme was that the child's non-eating was a defensive barrier. What emerged was the fear of eating which could result in the refusal of food. When the child, with full awareness, accepted food despite some fears, without any or very little defensive behaviour, then the first steps towards a meaningful, accepting, taking-in experience had been taken.

FUNCTIONAL LEARNING

In 1976, Dr Stroh met Dr Geoffrey Waldon, a neurologist who had worked in Manchester University for many years developing his educational theories, until eventually working in his own practice with developmentally delayed children. It was a meeting of minds, and the two exchanged ideas about early learning in relation to children with developmental delay. The result in practice was to give a new perspective and focus to the existing educational and learning work of the unit, helping to systematize what was already being done. It marked the beginning of what became known as Functional Learning.

Waldon (1985) said, 'Childhood is a period of preparation for survival as an independent and interdependent member of society.' It was also his idea (1966) that, 'the same adaptive mechanisms which normally maintain the child within its proper "normal" course-limits and encourage the continuity, proliferation and exploitation of learning may [also] operate to maintain a child in some widely divergent course, to retard and narrow the form as well as restrict the utilisation of any experience gained.' This is what happens when the effort a child normally uses to explore is misdirected into what becomes hyperactivity. By this misuse of effort, the child keeps other people at a distance and, at the same time, restricts experience. Similarly, the normal development of the use of tools enables a child to use a spoon in feeding and to get something out of a deep jar, but this can be misdirected, so, for example, the child may constantly flick the spoon. A precocious skill can be developed, such as the ability to spin objects, another example of a divergent course and a narrowing of experience.

1.4 PUTTING THEORY INTO PRACTICE

Functional Learning is learning for living with its difficulties and pleasures, its activities and times of rest. The best way to see the theory in practice is therefore to follow a child through their day at High Wick.

GETTING UP

To move from the safe world of bed into the complexity of daily life was difficult for many of the children. Children were in family groups with two care workers. A child was therefore helped into the new day by familiar adults, so keeping some things constant in a changing world. The care worker knew the child's level of learning and, in Functional Learning terms, understood the development of Learning Tools. So, for example, they knew if the child could sort appropriate clothes and sequence them in the right order, and whether they had the placing ability to put the clothes on. The care worker was also aware of any fears the child might have in either taking clothes off or putting them on. These fears were to be faced in as calm an atmosphere as possible, within the context of the child's increasing understanding.

SCHOOL

Each child belonged to one of three school groups which were organized according to level of development rather than chronological age. The childcare workers participated in the school groups as teaching assistants. The principles of Functional Learning and the Learning Tools (see 3.2) were common ground, enabling all the children to begin to understand the world around them. A great deal of thought was given to providing an appropriate learning environment, reducing sensory input where necessary, both in the way the classroom was set up and the way activities were presented to the child. The aim was to provide learning opportunities within the competence of each child, so that they did not need their secondary defensive behaviours and could discover the pleasure of taking in new learning and experience without fear. The teacher kept the environment safe, while the child worked at an uncluttered table with a clearly presented activity, being given appropriate help where necessary.

MEALTIMES

Similar Functional Learning principles operated at mealtimes. The dining table was uncluttered; the atmosphere was calm and quiet. Food was in tureens so that the children could be given small portions, but could also see that there was more when they wanted it. As a result, they were helped to take in food just as in school they had taken in learning. This taking-in became a pleasure rather than a fearful experience which needed to be defended against.

FREE TIME

There was plenty of opportunity outside school time and the daily routines for the children to be involved in doing other things. There was no division between work and play but simply a continual, active 'doing'. The children often spent time with staff in the unit. Being in the laundry was a favourite, as well as being in the kitchen with the cooks, or around the building with the cleaners – all of whom were using their learning tools to carry out their various functions!

There was outdoor play on swings and slides, and the children discovered that learning to place their body in space could be fun.

OUTINGS AND SPECIAL ACTIVITIES

At times a child would have a special time with their care worker or teacher. One of the favourite activities was cooking, in which the child needed to be able to place, sequence and use different utensils. At the same time there was an opportunity to explore the transformation which takes place when food is cooked. Shopping was another activity, usually at the village shop, which meant leaving the familiar and relatively 'safe' environment to enter the unpredictable world outside High Wick. All of this learning was learning for living, using the foundation of learning provided by the Functional Learning programmes to be able to integrate and function in the world outside High Wick.

NORMAL LIFE

The daily life described no doubt sounds like the normal life of any child. This is because Functional Learning is based on normal child development, using the knowledge of what normally developing children do, and how they learn, to help the developmentally delayed child to realize their potential.

1.5 FUNCTIONAL LEARNING

The integrated approach of Functional Learning clearly had its origins in the work that was done at High Wick Hospital during the 1960s and 1970s. The main features of the approach grew out of the research studies that were carried out and the daily care and learning programmes for the children:

- providing an appropriate environment
- emphasis on the potential for normal development and learning
- reducing the need for secondary defence behaviours
- the importance of feeding
- dealing with the emotional life of the child and family.

2

Play and Learning

CONTENTS

♦ Play in early childhood

♦ Observing early play in infants

♦ Links with learning and the Learning Tools

♦ Social play of the older child

♦ Play, learning and the development of understanding

♦ Play and learning of children with developmental delay

♦ Providing an appropriate environment

2.1 PLAY IN EARLY CHILDHOOD

'Descriptions of children's activities from a wide range of contemporary cultures suggest that play and playful childhood activities are part of all human societies' (Lindon, 2001). A great deal has been written about children's play from many different perspectives – historical, cultural, developmental and educational. In fact, looking through the literature on play, it can seem as if there are as many ideas about children's play as there are people writing about it. There are descriptions of physical play, solitary play, cooperative play, imaginative play, pretend play, outdoor play, playing games, social play, and play therapy. The focus on play particularly during the 20th century has attempted to describe and categorize play and otherwise to understand its function. There seems to be a general consensus that play and learning are inextricably linked. Evidence from neuroscience now suggests that play experiences from the age of two months, coinciding with an intense brain growth spurt, are central to development (Schore, 2001). But although there is agreement about the value of children's play, there are still differing ideas about the nature of play and how children learn through play.

Frances Salo (2005) makes the observation that babies need to be able to play alone to develop a true sense of self, and it is when they begin to feel confidence in themselves that the capacity to play alone appears. Although there are many ways of describing the play of young children, there does seem to be agreement about the qualities or characteristics of play. Play is cross-cultural. It is a pleasurable and self-motivated activity, done for its own sake and not to achieve some end purpose. It is quiet, effortful and can be repetitive. Children at play can be very absorbed, concentrating intently. Lois Bloom (1993) refers to 'quiet alert states … generally considered to be the moments during which infants are perceiving and learning from objects and events in their environment.'

2.2 OBSERVING EARLY PLAY IN INFANTS

Personal observations have shown that the play of normal infants reflects these qualities. The play of children under the age of two is closely linked to their physical development. Once they gain increasing bodily control and hand–eye coordination develops, their range of exploratory play is extended as they reach out, touch and grasp objects in their immediate environment. This was clearly seen when three normal infants, Katie, Sam and Eleanor, were followed up and filmed from five months to two years. The children were observed individually. They were each given a treasure basket of household and everyday objects (Forbes, 2004; Goldschmied and Jackson, 2003; Hughes, 2006). The basket was placed on the floor within easy reach of the infant, once they were able to sit up supported by cushions. A known adult was nearby so the infant felt safe and secure, but they did not participate in this independent play.

None of the infants had seen the basket of objects before. The response of each of the five-month-old babies was dramatic, and although they each had their own style of response, their activity with the objects was remarkably similar. Each baby leaned forward eagerly, practically falling over with excitement, eager to touch and then pick up the objects. The video of each of the babies showed that this interest and burst of activity continued for many minutes, as they repeatedly picked up, briefly examined and sometimes mouthed the objects, then let go. Sometimes an infant grasped one object in one hand and reached forward to pick up a second object with the other hand, perhaps shaking and accidentally hitting one object against the other. The pleasure the babies experienced encouraged them to repeat the action. This exploratory play was continuous and quiet, without the use of language, although each of the babies at five months had started to babble a little. The play of these babies showed the beginning of picking up, Placing and Banging, which are the earliest Learning Tools.

The treasure basket was given to each of the children at regular intervals, with a larger basket and more material in it as the babies grew and their physical ability increased, so that they were better coordinated, could reach further and hold objects for longer. At ten months, Eleanor, who is featured in the video on the CD, chose to take out a stick with several thick, coloured, circular shapes with holes which she had not played with before. She explored it by holding the stick in one hand while putting the shapes on and taking them off the stick with the other hand. Sometimes she changed hands but she was busy with this activity for over 20 minutes. She repeatedly pulled the shapes part way up the stick and let them drop down again, as if she liked the noise they made. When she noticed the holes in these circular shapes, she tried to see if the stick would go through the holes or the holes would go over the stick.

At 14 months, when all of the babies were already walking, the treasure basket was replaced with a small stroller, with handle and wheels, to put the objects in. Sometimes the infants enjoyed pushing the stroller around before sitting down beside it to play with the objects. For example, Katie took some wooden balls out and started rolling them across the floor one by one, then, picking up one in either hand she showed them in triumph to her mother, saying 'balls'. Katie was picking up and pairing and beginning to label objects.

The last recording of each of the children was at two years old, when the play materials were put on a small table and the child stood at the table to play and explore. There was a container of bricks which Sam tipped out onto the table, and then started picking them up and putting them back in the container. He repeated this activity with the balls on sticks, taking them off the sticks and putting them in a different container. Eleanor at two years chose to play with a wooden roundabout with horses. She found some wooden men, and the video shows her standing up at the table putting the men on the horses. At this age, Eleanor was talking, and while she played with the roundabout she described what she was doing, saying 'That one go there'. For both these children, their picking up and placing was well established and they showed early separating out which is the beginning of object sorting.

2.3 LINKS WITH LEARNING AND THE ▬ LEARNING TOOLS

Early play with objects is described here in terms of Learning Tools, a concept originally developed by Waldon. Observation clearly showed that normal babies under the age of two years freely explore their environment, meeting motor, perceptual and emotional needs. During the early pre-verbal exploration of Sam, Katie and Eleanor, their body activity was characterized by self-motivation, continuity, effort, quietness, endless repetition and pleasure with no sense of failure, all of which resulted in increasing competence. Out of this unspecific body activity, patterns began to emerge. These patterns of behaviour are the Learning Tools, mental or cognitive tools used by all children, cross-culturally, to learn and solve problems. The tools are Placing, Piling, Banging, Pairing, Matching, Sorting, Sequencing and Brick Building. The development of early play and learning in the young child is a highly complex process. The Learning Tools are interrelated and interdependent; they are rarely seen in isolation. They are sometimes seen in parallel, sometimes they overlap, sometimes they seem to merge, but they are always identifiable in the early play and learning of the very young child. Sam, Katie and Eleanor in their early play under two years already showed the beginnings of picking up, Placing, Pairing and Sorting.

2.4 SOCIAL PLAY OF THE OLDER CHILD

Once young children start to understand and use language, the early self-motivated play changes, as they become aware of the influence of others and the social rewards from parents and other adults. They use language in their play, communicating with other children and adults, imitating and sharing. Some of the early effects of interaction will reflect the culture and individual personalities of the parents and accepted ways of behaving. Social play takes place in the nursery and at school as well as at home, with friends and on the sports ground.

Wherever there are children, they will be playing. The children's games gradually become more competitive and associated with individual praise. Rules are introduced to clarify how these games are to be played with groups and teams. Play is becoming cooperative, only sometimes solitary, such as throwing a ball against a wall or kicking a football, but is still associated with pleasure, though less so for children who are sensitive or feel a failure, being less competent but wanting to win. Emotions in the playground are often intense, with some children showing how upset they are because they have not been chosen to be in a group.

2.5 PLAY, LEARNING AND THE DEVELOPMENT OF UNDERSTANDING

As Moyles (2005) has said, particularly in the last decade the association between play and learning has been clearly recognized by early years practitioners in childcare and education. Whitebread (1996) believes the key to this vital link lies in the qualities of children's play. He says, 'Observation of children at play gives some indication of why it might be such a powerful learning medium. During play children are usually totally engrossed in what they are doing. It is quite often repetitive and contains a strong element of practice. During play children set their own level of challenge, and so what they are doing is always developmentally appropriate (to a degree which tasks set by adults will never be). Play is spontaneous and initiated by the children themselves; in other words, during play children are in control of their own learning.'

He also says that, 'it is now widely accepted that children learn by a process of actively constructing their own understandings'. This statement encapsulates what Waldon had to say 15 years earlier about the development of understanding. This passage from the text of his video, *Understanding Understanding*, conveys the essence of his ideas about play, learning and understanding, in his description of two-year-old Jimmy playing by himself in the garden while his father is working nearby.

> Look at Jimmy playing. He's learning about himself and about the world. He's learning to understand. He's been playing by himself like this for ages. No one is directing his attention to the materials. No one is deliberately encouraging him to play. No one is telling him he's doing it properly. No one is praising his successes and no one is explaining anything and yet he's learning. He's learning very effectively and, what is more, he's learning how to learn even better in the future.
>
> In this kind of experience-gaining the child needs no one, he does everything himself. He chooses the behaviour from his store of experience. He initiates the action [and] it is reinforced by the pleasure he has taken in it. Whatever he does is good, so even if what happens is not quite what he intended it is still good. Everything new he learns now grows out of his attempts to do something he has done before and contains the essence of what has gone before. The richer the earlier understanding is the more likely it is to prove fundamentally valuable.
>
> Jimmy's playing and learning all by himself. Other people need [only to be somewhere nearby] when he plays like this. However, when he interacts socially with other people the forms of his learning and the kinds of understanding which result are quite different … within this, the social situation, the environment can play a major part in shaping the child's behaviour by heavily reinforcing selected responses deliberately, if not always consciously. Under these conditions Jimmy is learning the kinds of skills and information that his particular culture considers to be good for him.
>
> Our child through his play is constantly increasing his experience and organizing it into a general understanding which will guide his future actions, an understanding which is essentially similar to that of all other children. When he learns in association with other humans he tends to learn the sorts of skills which he shares only with those of the same or related cultures. These two very different kinds of understanding develop under differing sets of circumstances, the one where the child is effectively alone, the other under relatively social conditions. (Waldon, 1981)

The distinction that Waldon was making between what he refers to as general and particular understanding, and his description of non-social and social learning, have important implications for Functional Learning, because it informs this approach to helping developmentally delayed children with their play and learning.

2.6 PLAY AND LEARNING OF CHILDREN WITH ■ DEVELOPMENTAL DELAY

Before describing this approach in more detail, it is important to look at the play and learning of children with developmental delay. When development does not progress as expected in the young infant, delay occurs in sensory, motor, perceptual and emotional systems. There are many reasons why this can happen, including prematurity; genetic, neurological, bio-physiological, multi-system developmental disorders; language and communication disorders; emotional problems; and autistic spectrum disorders.

When the parents of a child with developmental delay are first seen, they often say that their child does not play, so they are already aware of this difference. These children do not show the early picking up and putting in, with objects and containers, which normally happens under the age of two. Some children use objects obsessively, for example always lining them up in the same way. They do not engage in the spontaneous, flexible, effortful activity so characteristic of the normally developing child. This lack of early exploratory play limits the establishment of the early Learning Tools. In addition, language has been slow to develop and understanding is often severely limited.

Because of the limitations in their early learning, understanding and coping strategies, these children resort to defensive behaviours to protect themselves against their fears and anxieties. These can be described as 'handicapping behaviours' because they further interfere with the child's development. When they find themselves in situations which make them fearful or anxious, and when they are overwhelmed by things they are unable to do or understand, these children show a range of responses, including retreating, screaming, crying, even in extreme cases spitting, scratching, biting and throwing things. Very often, parents have reached the end of their resources by the time they seek help.

2.7 PROVIDING AN APPROPRIATE ENVIRONMENT

There is general recognition that one of the essential factors in providing for children's play and learning is a suitable environment. 'When adults provide a varied play environment with opportunities to learn in all the different ways, they enable children to achieve some of the early learning goals' (Bruce, 2001). This is particularly important when considering children with developmental delay or other children with special needs.

Montessori, who initially worked with deprived children, was one of the first child educators to understand the importance of providing an appropriate environment and materials – the prepared environment – for children to be able to play and learn successfully. Anna Freud carried out psychoanalytical sessions for disturbed children in a quiet setting, with a single box full of chosen toys. Theraplay, developed by Ann Jernberg and Phyllis Booth (1999), uses the games and play activities of early infancy in a simple, uncluttered room, attempting to replicate healthy parent–child interaction to help children with emotional, behavioural and relationship problems. Stanley Greenspan devised 'Floor Time', which involves getting down on the floor with the child, interacting and playing, 'mobilizing intellectual and emotional growth in children with special needs' (Greenspan and Wieder, 1998).

In common with all of these practitioners and therapists, the aim of Functional Learning is to provide a therapeutic environment. The idea is to reproduce as closely as possible the conditions under which the normal young child plays and learns, based on the development of the Learning Tools. The guiding principles of other approaches are similar, and there is an overlap in terms of providing an appropriate environment for the development of play and learning, but this is only one part of the overall integrative approach of Functional Learning.

Functional Learning

CONTENTS

- Functional Learning defined

- Learning, emotions and neuroscience

- Facilitation of the Learning Tools

- Secondary defensive behaviour

- How to set up Functional Learning sessions

- The emotional dimension

- Frequency of the learning sessions

- Use of video

- Adapting Functional Learning to different children

- Functional Learning and educational initiatives

3.1 FUNCTIONAL LEARNING DEFINED

The term 'Functional Learning' evolved from the work at High Wick Hospital and the working collaboration between George Stroh and Geoffrey Waldon in the 1970s (see 1.3). Waldon had used the term 'fundamental general understanding' to refer to the experience gained from self-motivated, effortful, independent, pleasurable early play and exploration carried out under what he termed 'a-social' or non-social conditions; he regarded this experience as the basis of all future learning. Stroh wanted to broaden the term. 'Functional', to paraphrase the Oxford Dictionary (*The Concise Oxford Dictionary of Current English*, 1995), refers to a special kind of activity that fulfils its purpose. It was this idea of activity with a purpose that Stroh wanted to convey. So the term Functional Learning was adopted to describe the unique integrative approach that was developed with its focus on the facilitation of the early Learning Tools, while recognizing the vital importance of emotional development.

The work of Greenspan and colleagues in the USA, who also use the term functional, is perhaps closest to the therapeutic intervention of Functional Learning in helping children with developmental delay and their parents. 'The infant or young child's functional emotional developmental level reveals how the child uses everyday functioning to integrate all capacities (social, motor, cognitive, language, spatial, and sensory) to carry out emotionally meaningful (i.e. functional) goals ... We call the six core capacities "functional" for two reasons. First, they enable the child to interact with and comprehend his or her world. Second, they orchestrate many other capabilities' (Greenspan and Wieder, 2006). Through research and observation of many different kinds of developmental problems, a new way of working has been developed, providing a comprehensive developmental approach and a therapeutic intervention tailored to the needs of each individual child. Both approaches acknowledge the interdependence of emotional and cognitive growth. The difference is one of emphasis.

3.2 LEARNING, EMOTIONS AND NEUROSCIENCE

In acknowledging the importance of the emotional life of the child, Functional Learning reflects recent research in neuroscience demonstrating the vital link between cognitive and emotional processes. It has been recognized that emotion plays a critical part in learning, reasoning and creativity and in organizing and integrating brain function (Damasio, 1998; Gerhardt, 2004; Siegel, 1999). Information from clinical practice is being considered alongside scientific evidence, and ideas about 'feelings ... and the critical significance of early developmental experience', which have usually been the concern of psychotherapy, are informing scientific research (Carroll, 2003). In particular, Allan Schore (2001) has been instrumental in bringing together Bowlby's ideas on attachment and data from brain research, suggesting that 'the early social–emotional interaction between the primary caregiver and the infant impacts the development of the baby's brain.'

3.3 FACILITATION OF THE LEARNING TOOLS

CONDITIONS FOR LEARNING

It may be useful at this point to remind ourselves of the characteristics of early play and learning:

- Early pre-verbal play is self-motivated.
- No, or very little, language is used.

- This play is quiet, effortful, and repetitive and carried out with concentration.

- There is no fear of failure.

- There is not necessarily an end goal – the activity is carried out for its own sake.

- Pleasure is intrinsic – there is no training, cajoling or social reward.

- The adult simply provides a safe, supportive environment.

Functional Learning simulates as closely as possible the experience of the normal young child during self-motivated play, where learning is non-social, open-ended, not dependent on rewards and largely free from language direction. It offers a range of learning activities for the delayed child, to facilitate the Learning Tools within the structure of individual learning sessions. Once the earliest Learning Tools become established, parents will be able to provide their child with many opportunities within the home environment for 'doing' and exploring. As the child's curiosity and self-motivation begin to grow, with parents' emotional support, play does become a pleasurable, shared experience.

THE LEARNING ENVIRONMENT

Although initially the learning sessions take place under controlled conditions, they are part of a multi-dimensional dynamic process that provides for great flexibility and creative opportunities to extend and vary activities once the child is settled. On the CD, you can see children sitting at the table working, with practitioners and parents helping them. The following guidelines will help you to provide an appropriate learning environment for Functional Learning sessions:

- Ideally, you need a quiet workroom for the individual learning sessions or, within a classroom, a work station if possible as described in Chapter 20.3. For the learning sessions at home, parents will need to organize a special workspace, which could be in the child's bedroom.

- You need a working table that is wide enough and long enough for the child to be able to reach to full arm's length in all directions, to help the child develop a wide range of body movement and to encourage maximum effort.

- It is helpful if the table is placed facing an empty wall to cut down distractions, to allow the child to focus on the learning activities.

- The chair should be an appropriate size for the individual child.

- For the smaller child, you can put a stool under the child's feet so that they can feel safe, supported and contained at the table.

- You need to sit just behind or to one side of the child, so that the child's focus is the activity on the table. This also makes it easier to help the child by guiding their hands if necessary.

- The materials for the activities are prepared before the session so that you do not need to move away from the table. Any movement can distract the vulnerable child who may also feel anxious if you move away and the flow of the activity is interrupted.

- Later on, when the child is competent enough to work alone, there will be times when you can move away while the child continues to work independently.

- The activities are continuous, like the activity of the typical young child playing, without a sense that it's moving towards an end. Within each activity, the same materials are often used in different ways, and one activity flows into the next, building up the child's interest, concentration and motivation.

- Verbal instructions or explanations are kept to a minimum during the learning activities, so that the child can concentrate on what they are doing. Some simple language can be added later, when appropriate, once the child's understanding begins to develop.

- It is not necessary to say 'no' or 'that's wrong', but to be supportive of the child's efforts. Just like the early play and learning of the normal infant, everything the child does is good when working at the activities, trying to understand and solve problems.

- Praise or other rewards are not used while the child is working. The focus is always on the doing, and sometimes a few simple words can be used to convey this to the child, such as 'This is for you', 'It's your work', or 'You are learning'.

3.4 SECONDARY DEFENSIVE BEHAVIOUR

Change is difficult for children with developmental delay and produces feelings of discomfort. During the initial new physical experience of sitting on a chair, the child's secondary defensive behaviours may increase. These can include anything from constantly asking for a favourite toy or a drink of water to actual physical withdrawal, pushing things off the table, or screaming, raging and attacking. It is not always easy, but it is important to try to remain calm and tolerant in the knowledge that the child's strong feelings of unease and discomfort are a reaction to having to change their familiar patterns of behaviour. Avoiding confrontation or punishment, but staying with the child, helping them to remain at the table and to use the learning materials, sets limits which will also give them a sense of security.

There are various strategies that can be used to help lower tensions and anxieties, so that the child finds it less necessary to resort to these maladaptive responses, releasing more of their energies for the Functional Learning activities. Observing the child's body cues and making immediate changes in the work if they show signs of anxiety, agitation or distress – perhaps returning to an earlier, more familiar activity or reducing the amount of materials – allows the child to settle and carry on. Sometimes for the very young child who is upset and crying, if the parents are there, the work can be stopped and the child settled on the parent's lap for a short time, until they can gradually be helped back to the chair once they feel safe.

Gradually the child does settle down, finding that under these special conditions the secondary defensive behaviours are no longer effective and are in fact quite unnecessary. Parents may find it harder at home to manage the resistance, when their child may try to pull their hands away or push things on the floor, which is often very upsetting. But they do find ways of coping, sometimes rather unexpected ones. The parents of one child said they found their son's resistance so intolerable they started to throw beanbags at each other!

3.5 HOW TO SET UP FUNCTIONAL LEARNING SESSIONS

THE MATERIALS

Children with developmental delay are limited in their play and generally do not use a wide range of traditional toys or play materials to explore and learn. Functional Learning activities create opportunities for these children to begin to learn and solve problems, giving them the Learning Tools to explore their environment. Apart from large wooden bricks which usually need to be bought – though there are schools and families who have made their own – the Functional Learning sessions use common everyday objects found in the immediate environment and familiar to most children. As the children progress and develop, there is a need to extend the activities; one of the ways of doing this is to use card material. Many examples of the learning materials and a range of cards are illustrated on the CD.

In the clinic or classroom setting or at home, it is important to have some way of storing and organizing the materials that will be used for the special learning sessions, either on open shelves or in a large cupboard with plenty of shelf space, so that they are always available when needed. Particularly for those children who may wander aimlessly, pulling things off shelves or out of cupboards, it is also a way of helping them to understand that you are looking after these special materials to help their learning, and that they are not to be broken or destroyed.

- Materials for each session are placed close to the working table, to be easily accessible.

- They may vary in amount or variety from session to session, but there will always be a few basic materials which are common to, and necessary for, every session.

- They include a number of plain wooden or plastic trays; small non-breakable dishes; a variety of containers such as boxes, bags and tins of different sizes, shapes and materials; and specially-made wooden boards for Pairing, Matching, Sorting and Sequencing.

- Collections of everyday objects as well as sets of cards can be kept ready for Pairing, Matching and Sorting, depending on the needs of the individual child.

- It is useful to keep a container of large wooden bricks to be used if the child's behaviour gives cause for concern. You can then help the child to continue working by switching to earlier well-known activities such as Placing with bricks.

USING CARDS

Sets of custom-made cards have an enormous variety of uses and many qualities that make them invaluable for Functional Learning activities.

- They fulfil the need to extend and practise using all the Learning Tools.

- They are convenient, do not take up a great deal of space and can easily be filed and stored so that they can be readily selected for immediate use.

- The 5 cm square cards that are used are a good size for even small children to handle.

- They can provide a wide selection of single-image information, from a simple black-and-white outline to the most complex coloured picture.

- They can help prepare the child for using books which can otherwise be overwhelming, with too much information.

- With a supply of blank cards always available, sets of cards can be made during the Functional Learning session to help extend an activity or to fill any information gaps for an individual child.

- They offer great flexibility – they can be used in individual sets or in combination with other sets or even with objects.

More details about using sets of cards can be found under the individual Learning Tools in Section II.

PLANNING THE LEARNING SESSIONS

Functional Learning sessions are designed to meet the needs of the individual child. Each session needs to follow a natural progression of activities, always working within the child's level of competence by giving them things they are familiar with and can do. This ensures the child's success and makes it unnecessary for them to fall back on the secondary defensive behaviours. Through constant repetition of things they can do, while all the time making small variations, chance things happen which lead to new learning and understanding.

It is important to be flexible and, although each session is planned in advance, changes may have to be made to meet the needs of the child at the time. The following plan for Functional Learning sessions is therefore only a suggested plan and will always need to take into account the immediate needs of the individual child. It is not meant to imply that each session covers all the activities – the intention is to illustrate a possible progression of activities, but where you start for each session and what you include will always depend on the child you are working with. Sometimes an entire session may focus on one of the Learning Tools; at other times you will use a range of activities for different Learning Tools.

The chapters in Section II describe specific activities for each of the Learning Tools. But there are certain general guidelines that apply regardless of the Learning Tools you are trying to facilitate.

- For children who are just beginning to establish the earliest Learning Tools, start with an activity that involves using large body movements such as placing bricks in buckets.

- You can extend this initial Placing, helping the child to use alternate hands for placing beanbags in large bowls.

- Banging with sticks is another activity that you can use to facilitate large body movements. Moving and stretching across the whole table increases the child's effort and range of movement.

- This can then lead on to scraping movements, extensive movements using sticks and then thick crayons, one in either hand, making marks on paper, stretching over the whole table.

- Continue with a variety of Placing activities, including placing rings on sticks, screwing and unscrewing large wooden screws, and putting objects such as pieces of a very simple puzzle in containers (zip bags, tins, boxes).

- If the child has not had much experience of handling objects, Piling activities offer plenty of opportunities for moving different materials around, where the interest is more in the doing than in the outcome. A variety of materials suitable for Piling can be kept in large containers, ready for piling on to a table and being moved around at random, exploring the different things that happen every time an object is moved.

- For the child who is ready, you can use an early Pairing activity with objects, after some initial Placing.

- Once Placing and Pairing are well established, Matching on the Matching board can be introduced, with objects then with cards.

- You can also include simple Sorting activities in the session, with objects first before moving gradually into Sorting with cards on the Sorting boards. Even when a child is Sorting with cards, object Sorting still continues, using increasingly complex sorting categories.

- After practice with the many learning activities to encourage the development of movement and exploration of space, children are ready to move on to Brick Building to extend their knowledge and understanding of spatial relationships.

- Some Sequencing is associated with Placing, in the sequence of actions involved in putting objects in containers, but you can now add activities to establish Sequencing as a Learning Tool.

- Once children can pair, match, sort and sequence and have begun to develop conceptual thinking, activities like Coding and Intersectional Sorting can be introduced, and eventually all of the Learning Tools can be extended onto worksheets.

ADDITIONAL ACTIVITIES

Once the child is settled and beginning to develop the earliest Learning Tools, other activities can be introduced, perhaps towards the end of a session. You can give the child a large container of mixed materials, similar to the treasure basket (Hughes, 2006) to encourage independent exploration and play. You might give the child some metal chains which they can put in and out of a selection of containers. You can use play dough to help the child roll, cut and make simple shapes with pastry cutters. If the child is beginning to make marks on paper spontaneously, you can give them thick crayons to produce their own drawing. Use large sheets of paper, providing a new sheet as soon as the child has covered the space or indicated that they need more.

At the end of a session, the child may want to return to some of the materials used during the learning activities – a positive response to the pleasure of doing and a move towards self-initiated and self-motivated play. The reward is in the activity and the bonus is the child wanting to continue. The goal is for the delayed child to learn, explore, play and understand for themselves. This is not dependent on social rewards from the adult. It is not necessary to praise the child during the session; it is more positive to offer more activities so the reward is in the pleasure of doing more. Although rewards and praise are not used, the adult's body language and, at times, a few appropriate words communicate to the child that they share the child's pleasure in the activities.

3.6 THE EMOTIONAL DIMENSION

The intensive Functional Learning work does not preclude the emotional dimension. It is important to be alert to the child's feelings, often reflected in their body language (Stroh and Robinson, 1988). They may stamp their feet, stiffen their arms, make their hands go floppy, slip under the table, throw things, grimace, make noises, or cry. You may need to change the focus of the session to deal with these feelings. You can move the child's chair so that they can see your face, which needs to remain calm and relaxed. Using very simple language, you can help them understand what is happening: these are baby feelings; you are sad; you feel hurt; you are a growing boy/girl; you can change those feelings; we can help your sad feelings; you are safe; the work is for you; mummy and daddy can help you too. Sharing these feelings and relieving the immediate distress allows the child to return to the activities on the table. Eventually, they will start to use their own words to describe their feelings instead of resorting to the early primitive body language.

3.7 FREQUENCY OF THE LEARNING SESSIONS

Functional Learning sessions last for one to two hours. For some children, an intensive six-month period of weekly sessions is followed by a period of monthly follow-up sessions. Other children, whose development is severely delayed, may need a more prolonged period of treatment. Once the programme is started, regular Functional Learning sessions at home are vital. A time needs to be set aside each day – half an hour to start with, extended to an hour or longer as parents become more familiar with the ideas.

3.8 USE OF VIDEO

An exchange of video is extremely helpful to the progress of the treatment programme. A video of a working session can be made at regular intervals and edited for parents to use at home, to help them continue the daily practice. For some families, distance therapy is an option, a combination of periodic intensive sessions over two to three days, supplemented by a video exchange between parents and therapist to monitor progress.

It is extremely hard work and very demanding of parents' time and energy. Parents have many different demands made on them, and may have to make some very difficult decisions in order to have time available for this vital therapeutic input for their child. But, of course, when they see their child's emerging learning and increased responsiveness, they are always encouraged to continue.

3.9 ADAPTING FUNCTIONAL LEARNING TO DIFFERENT CHILDREN

THE OLDER CHILD

Although the current work in neuroscience suggests that the brain organizes itself in response to input received very early in development, it also reports that learning does continue into later years. According to the neuroscientist, Jay Giedd (2002), research has revealed that the brain is extremely plastic. For some time it was thought that most things were set in place during the early years. But it is now known that there is enormous capacity for change throughout childhood and into the teen years.

Clinical experience shows that older children from seven years onwards with developmental delay can benefit from Functional Learning, but it takes longer to establish the Learning Tools. As children get older, any secondary defensive behaviours become more firmly established in response to their fear of failing, poor self-esteem and the often inappropriate expectations of the environment. These problem behaviours can become so pervasive that they obscure the developmental delay which is the primary problem. But if you can contain the strength and pain of the child, which may be more difficult because of the child's size, you can help them begin to channel these energies into the learning activities.

Some aspects of the Functional Learning environment and the learning materials may need to be modified. For example, you may need a much larger table and chair. To increase effort and range of movement proportional to body size, the child can stand up at the end of the table to extend their reach. You can provide heavier bricks, or even milk cartons filled with sand, for placing vigorously and continuously into a strong container. Picking up and placing can continue in the outside environment, by getting the child to carry buckets, filling them with stones or water for the garden. The child can help push a trolley in the supermarket, loading up the car with the heavy bags and taking them into the house. These activities will take practice but they will be within the competence of most children. Once the child begins to put their energy and effort into the Placing activities, taking pleasure in this kind of body movement, the secondary defensive behaviours will lessen. Other Functional Learning activities can then be provided, such as Piling, Banging, Pairing, Matching and Sorting, always at a pace suited to the individual child.

CHILDREN WITH MOVEMENT DISORDERS

Children with movement disorders such as cerebral palsy need a great deal of help to overcome difficulties in sensory processing and motor planning, in order to achieve the levels of self-regulation needed to successfully interact with and explore their environment. Young children with motor planning difficulties can be given Functional Learning activities by liaising closely with physiotherapists, whose experience of functional movement can be incorporated into the Functional Learning sessions.

3.10 FUNCTIONAL LEARNING AND EDUCATIONAL INITIATIVES

Functional Learning and its underlying philosophy that every child can learn fits in well with educational initiatives like Birth to Three Matters (Department for

Children, Schools and Families, 2002), Foundation Stage (Qualifications and Curriculum Authority, 2000) and Early Years Foundation Stage (Department for Education and Skills, 2007). There are common themes – the importance of a secure, loving relationship with parents and carers; an appropriate environment suited to children's changing learning needs as they grow and develop; the knowledge that children develop and learn in different ways and at their own pace; and agreement that all areas of development and learning are interconnected.

A brief survey of some of the central ideas indicates that there are many other ways in which Functional Learning principles coincide with these educational initiatives in providing for children's learning needs. Play underpins the development and learning of the young child. Through play, children explore and make sense of their world. These learning experiences help them to develop ideas and concepts, think creatively, and problem-solve, establishing a firm foundation for all future learning. Children learn by doing, developing their body coordination and control, fine movement and manipulation. Functional Learning, along with these initiatives, has similar things to say about the basis for the development of communication, reading, writing and number. Very young children use gesture and body language and, as they develop, their language and communication grows from their early play and learning. They also develop mathematical understanding through their early play experiences with shape, size, pattern, sorting, and matching.

Another theme in common, highlighted by the Social and Emotional Aspects of Learning (SEAL) framework (Department for Education and Skills, 2005), is the crucial importance of taking into account and supporting the emotional development of the child. It is accepted that the emotions play a central role in learning experiences. Helping children develop a sense of self, feel good about themselves, and understand their feelings and why they make them behave the way they do are all important to learning.

With so much in common, it means that Functional Learning can play an important role in helping children with developmental delay to establish a foundation of early play and learning, so that they can be supported in a similar way in nursery or school. For those children who are not yet able to take immediate advantage of the learning environment provided by a nursery or school setting within mainstream education, Functional Learning helps to establish their Learning Tools and support their emotional development so that they can begin to join in. It is possible to help an individual child using Functional Learning principles, within a nursery or school classroom, with the support of a teaching assistant as described in Chapter 20.

Assessment

CONTENTS

- Traditional assessment
- Diagnostic labels
- Initial assessment
- Assessment as an integral part of intervention

4.1 TRADITIONAL ASSESSMENT

Over the last decade, developmental specialists working with young children have begun to move away from traditional assessment, which attempted to predict future performance on the basis of current functioning (Bellman, 2001; Greenspan and Wieder, 1998; Meisels and Atkins-Burnett, 2000). This is in line with Functional Learning which acknowledges that every child has their own unique developmental pace. Children can find the experience of assessment in an unfamiliar environment, with someone they do not know, worrying and even frightening, particularly because the tests may be measuring skills they do not yet have. There is a range of tests – developmental checklists, behaviour rating scales, cognitive tests – that are appropriate for children who have learning, language and motor problems. They can be helpful in assessing children for nursery or school placement, and can be used most successfully after a child has been working for some time with Functional Learning and has begun to develop Learning Tools.

4.2 DIAGNOSTIC LABELS

Children are referred for various reasons – because they are not talking yet, their behaviour may be giving cause for concern, they may have feeding difficulties – and with various diagnoses – Down's syndrome, autistic spectrum disorder, cerebral palsy, hearing loss. In this book, the term 'developmental delay' has been used rather than looking at children in terms of diagnoses, disorders or syndromes, because each area of development is interlinked with and dependent on all other areas. Diagnostic labels can be useful but they can also be limiting in their focus and they do not necessarily take into account individual differences. Although parents may initially experience a sense of relief when given a label, for some parents it can lead to a loss of optimism for the potential of their child, as it may cause them to focus on the problems and difficulties and the things their child cannot do. Functional Learning looks at children from a developmental perspective, dealing with the whole child – their early learning and language development, their emotional growth and relationships within the family. Because all areas of development are interdependent, Functional Learning is an integrated therapeutic approach.

4.3 INITIAL ASSESSMENT

Whatever form an initial assessment takes in a Functional Learning setting, the aim is to start with things the child *can* do. This, combined with the fact that the child is seen with their parents, will help to reduce the fear and worry at having to meet people they do not know in an unfamiliar environment.

Creating an informal setting for the initial interview or assessment can further reduce any anxiety. A range of play material is available – large bricks, a selection of common objects, some containers, drawing materials, perhaps some simple games for the older children. From an observation of the child's responses to these materials, and interaction with their parents, it is possible to begin to get an idea of what Functional Learning activities will be appropriate to start with. Once the learning sessions begin, continued observation of the child over time will help to form an overall developmental profile, and it may then become evident that the child has specific problems in one particular area.

The format of the initial visit can vary, depending on the needs of each child and family. For some children, after an informal period at the start to become used to the environment and new people, it may be appropriate to introduce some more formal Functional Learning activities. How long this part of the initial visit lasts and how many Learning Tools are explored will depend on the close observation of the child by the practitioner. It is quite common to find that, because the child is being presented with things they can understand and can do, their concentration span is much greater than anticipated. This more formal presentation of Functional Learning activities can be a positive help to parents, who can see that their child is able to do things, and then feel encouraged to start a Functional Learning programme.

It is useful to make a short video during the initial visit which can be used as a baseline for comparison of future progress. A report can be prepared for parents based on observation of the child and information they have provided themselves, with a suggested plan for further sessions and a Functional Learning programme. With the agreement of the parents, the report can also be made available to others involved in the child's treatment and care.

4.4 ASSESSMENT AS AN INTEGRAL PART OF INTERVENTION

Assessment of the child needs to take place over a period of time and to become an integral part of treatment. As the Functional Learning practitioner works with a child, they are continually assessing where the child is in terms of the Learning Tools, communication skills and responsiveness to parents/carers and therapist. This means constantly adjusting the treatment programme to suit the changing needs of the child over time. Rather than a child being compared with other children, the child is compared with themselves, and where they were before. It may not be possible to predict the rate of progress and how far the child will close the gap. But what is known is that all children can learn, and each child has their own unique pace and learning style. Assessment and intervention become part of an ongoing process of observation, exchange of information with parents and any other professionals involved, and cueing in to the needs of the child. A brief description of Laura will show how this works in practice.

Laura was nearly five when she was first seen, referred because of her delayed learning and language and difficult behaviour. She was an only child, living with her mother who spoke about Laura's medical problems that needed constant follow-up hospital visits, with many different professionals involved.

During the initial interview which lasted an hour, Laura stayed close to her mother, only sitting on her own chair if her mother sat right next to her. She swung between trying to please and amuse and shouting and resisting any help. Although there were play materials available, she did not engage with anything for very long, finally putting her head on the table and folding her hands behind her neck. All the energy she used to protect herself with these secondary defensive behaviours was therefore not available for her own learning and understanding.

Laura attended a normal infant school and the school report which her mother provided said that she was not able to cope with the reading, writing and early number work, and that she had special learning needs different from the other children. The psychologist who had seen Laura on a number of occasions had tried very hard to be flexible, but had to conclude that Laura found the process of individual assessment very stressful because it highlighted her areas of difficulty – and she responded by withdrawing and avoiding the activity.

(Continued)

(Continued)

Laura's anxiety about separating from her mother and her uncertainty and lack of trust were not surprising in view of her history of frequent hospital visits. A second visit was arranged to see Laura's mother, to talk about the initial visit and to discuss future sessions. She was relieved to know that there would not be a formal assessment. The intervention for Laura needed to focus on helping her to feel safe enough to separate from her mother. She would be given Functional Learning activities within her level of competence so that she could begin to feel successful. Some simple language would be used to help her understand her feelings in the context of her daily difficulties.

During six months of weekly sessions, as the loud, aggressive defensive behaviour began to fall away, an extremely vulnerable, sensitive little girl with good learning potential began to emerge. She was able to separate from her mother and to sit working at the table for most of an hour's session. Once she had become more settled in the sessions, Laura showed an increasing level of competence with the early learning activities, although her overall ability was not age-appropriate. She was picking up and placing, pairing, matching and sorting. Her language improved dramatically, her words and sentence structure, though simple, were appropriate and she used the personal pronouns. But whenever her anxiety rose, the secondary defensive behaviour reappeared, her competence dropped and her language reverted to being stereotyped and repetitive, mainly used as a defence. By observing Laura during this time, so that she could be given appropriate activities to establish her Learning Tools, it had become clear that this was not a primary language problem but part of an overall developmental delay with associated emotional difficulties.

SECTION II

DEVELOPMENT OF THE LEARNING TOOLS

This gives a comprehensive description of all the Learning Tools – Placing, Piling, Banging and Drawing, Pairing, Matching, Sorting, Sequencing and Brick Building. Each chapter is devoted to one of the Learning Tools, with extensive details of the practical activities that can be used to help children with developmental delay. This in-depth information will enable practitioners and parents to set up Functional Learning sessions. Understanding of the development of the Learning Tools will come through carrying out these activities.

The Placing Tool

CONTENTS

- What is Placing?

- Body awareness and sense of self

- Placing and children with developmental delay

- Use of the guiding hand

- Materials used for Placing

- Simple Placing

- Intermediate Placing

- Mature Placing

- Placing in everyday life

5.1 WHAT IS PLACING?

Placing is an essential component of the fundamental learning process and the ability to physically explore the environment; it is a prerequisite for all the Learning Tools and it is used throughout life. Placing involves picking things up and putting them down. The earliest Placing is associated with feeding and the breast or bottle in the mouth. The baby's continuous mouthing of objects gradually changes from exploring with the mouth to using the hands, picking things up and letting them go, at first unintentionally.

From about six months onwards, the baby begins to look at and reach for objects, at first close to their own body and gradually further away. By the end of the first year, both sides of the body are already working together, the baby can focus attention over a wide area and, in more complex activities, the hands begin to complement each other. Early in the second year, the young infant begins to move objects successively from one place to another, often placing objects one by one into a container, 'the rhythmically progressive sequential behaviour' that Waldon (1988) called continuant activity.

5.2 BODY AWARENESS AND SENSE OF SELF

Placing activities are closely associated with body awareness. Infants are placed in their surroundings, becoming aware of the space around them through bodily movements. They learn what the body will do, and about its size and other characteristics in relation to their surroundings, when changing position from lying down to sitting, crawling, standing, reaching and picking up objects. Through body movement and exploration of the environment, they develop a growing understanding of themselves in space. As the baby begins to discover that they can move and do things, they are also learning about 'me' and 'not me'. 'In the spatula game, Winnicott had noted the infant's early use of what he called a Not-me-possession' (Phillips, 1988). He describes a baby sitting on the mother's lap being attracted to a shiny metal spatula, reaching out for it, but hesitating until the feeling of wanting the spatula made the baby pick it up and start mouthing, banging and playing with it.

As babies act on the environment, they experience the consequences of their actions. If things are moved, then things happen and, of course, what actually happens may be different from what was expected – in other words, learning takes place. 'Learning is certainly not designed for the exclusive purpose of forming a sense of self, but a sense of self will be one of the many vital byproducts of the general learning capacity' (Stern, 1985).

5.3 PLACING AND CHILDREN WITH DEVELOPMENTAL DELAY

Children with developmental delay have a range of problems, often multi-causal, that can interfere with motor, perceptual and spatial development. Many of these children dislike any change in the environment and do not touch or explore objects freely. Some become obsessed with one object so their exploration and learning is limited. Delayed children usually do not engage in self-motivated play. They do not reach out to their surroundings but either remain passive or move around rapidly, so there is little opportunity for sustained experience of picking up and placing.

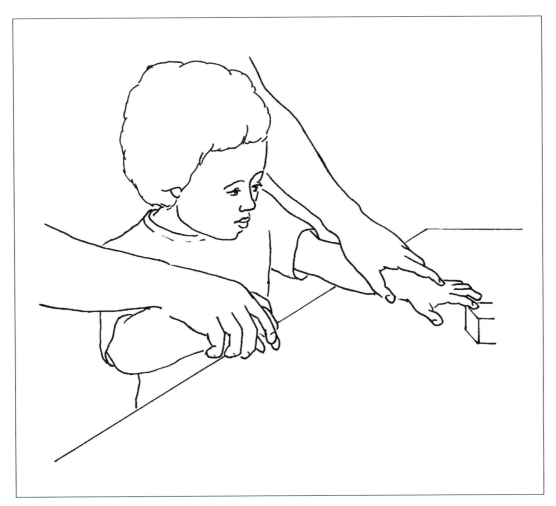

FIGURE 1 GUIDING A CHILD'S HANDS.

5.4 USE OF THE GUIDING HAND

Children who have had limited experience of picking up and exploring objects can feel anxious and fearful when faced with new situations. Because of their limited understanding, they become agitated, passive or angry (see 3.4 on secondary defensive behaviour). These feelings are often expressed during the early Placing activities and they may cry or scream. By staying with the child and continuing with the activity, you can help to contain their feelings until the rhythm of their body movement begins to take over, and they begin to settle down, shifting their focus to what they are doing. In the unfamiliar working environment of the Functional Learning sessions, you can guide the child's hands to help them overcome their fears. Your hands are placed over the child's hands, holding them firmly but flexibly, so that they almost become an extension of the child's hand, as Figure 1 shows. By observing the child's behaviour and feeling their hands moving under yours, you can decide

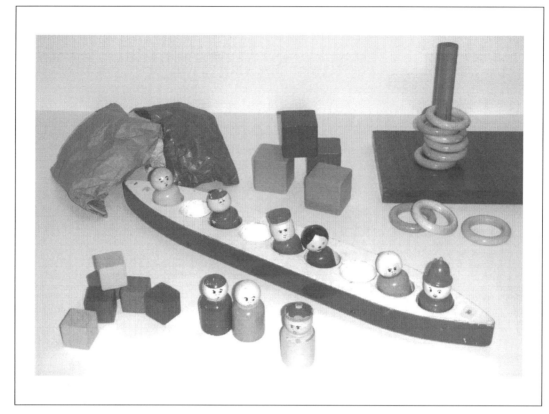

FIGURE 2 MATERIALS FOR PLACING.

when to gently withdraw your hands so that the child can work alone for short periods.

5.5 MATERIALS USED FOR PLACING

There are two basic types of early Placing activities and many variations of both. The first is picking up an object and placing it somewhere else – usually in a container of some sort. The second is placing an object via an obstruction, such as a bag, a jar, or a tin. You need relatively large objects and containers to help develop large body movements, and a range of other materials to help develop finer movements and particularly finger–thumb opposition. Some of the materials are shown in Figure 2.

Much of the initial Placing is done with wooden bricks, preferably not coloured, and not too large for the small child's hands but large enough for the older child with larger hands. To encourage effortful activity in the older child, the bricks will need to be heavier; if bricks are not heavy enough, special containers can be made and filled with sand. In addition to bricks, you can use large beanbags for this first energetic Placing. You also need several large containers, such as plastic bowls, for placing things in.

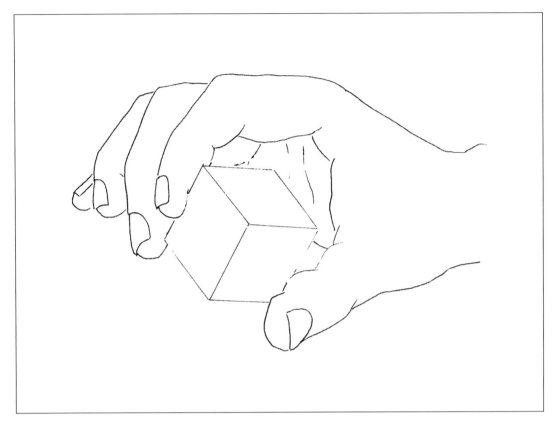

FIGURE 3 FINGER-THUMB OPPOSITION.

For intermediate Placing, rings on sticks and wooden balls on sticks can be used in many different ways. Another useful piece of equipment, which can be made, is a solid wooden base with holes for six or eight upright wooden cylinders. Montessori cylinder blocks and wooden men in boats are examples of commercially available equipment that can be used for these Placing activities. Very small bricks of about 1–1.5 cm square are used for picking up and placing to develop finger–thumb opposition, as Figure 3 shows. And, finally, for obstruction Placing, a mature Placing activity, you need a selection of things like bags with different types of fastenings, jars, boxes and tins. Many of the materials that can be used for Placing activities are illustrated on the CD.

5.6 SIMPLE PLACING

Simple Placing activities are designed to facilitate movements that promote bodily integration, so that the different parts of the body begin to work in harmony, enabling the child to concentrate and focus their attention. Repetitive, continuous, effortful placing encourages the child to reach out and stretch as far as possible using both hands, while visually following the movement, and to switch attention from one side of the body to the other.

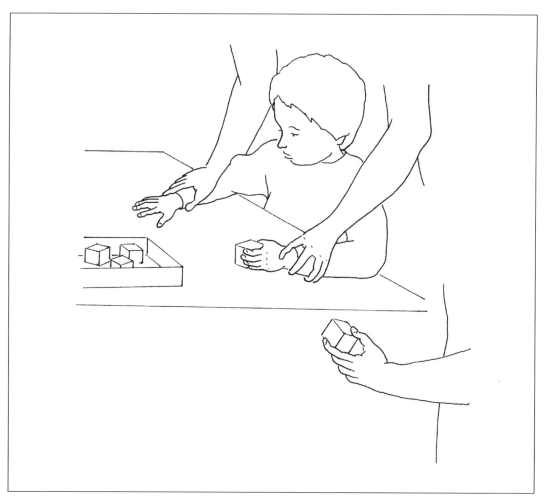

FIGURE 4 SIMPLE PLACING WITH BRICKS.

- Put a large plastic bowl or similar container on the table, positioned so that the child has to stretch to reach it.

- Begin the activity by putting a brick on the table just in front of the child, guiding the child's hand to pick up and place the brick in the container, as shown in Figure 4. The other hand is left free on the table with a guiding hand held over it to keep it still, to help the child focus on the movement of placing the brick in the container. Some children leave their other hand down at their side or on their lap under the table, as if they only had one hand. If this happens, help them to bring their other hand up to rest on the table, if appropriate using a few simple words, such as 'You need this hand too'. This helps to increase the awareness of both sides of the body.

- Present the bricks continuously, one at a time, guiding the child's hand to pick up and place each one, vigorously and with effort.

- Do the placing with the child's other hand, and continue placing like this a number of times, with each hand in turn.

- Change to placing with alternate hands, guiding the child's hands to pick up and place a brick with one hand and then the other hand, rhythmically and energetically.

- Begin to introduce variations, putting the bricks in different places on the table, at various distances from the child, but still presenting them one at a time. When the position of the brick changes, the child has to look for it each time before reaching for it, picking it up, and placing it in the container.

- Put the container in different places on the table – in the middle, to one side, to the other side – which means the child experiences moving in as many different directions as possible.

- If the child is not looking in the direction of the container, then move the container further away. The more the child has to stretch to reach it, the more likely it is that their eyes will follow their hand.

- Hold the container above the table, sometimes moving it nearer or further away, to one side or the other, even behind the child who will need to look upwards, move round and stretch to place each brick.

- Increase the amount of material and speed of delivery to increase effort and attention/concentration.

- Introduce different objects for this simple Placing, using beanbags and even pine cones if they are available.

For these early Placing activities, although it is possible to work on your own, it is preferable to work together with a helper to manage the materials and keep the continuity going, by placing the bricks or other objects on the table and moving the container. This will allow the person who is guiding the child's hands to focus on the child's responses.

Once the child shows increasing competence in the initial Placing activities, you can spread the bricks all over the table and encourage both continuity of picking up and placing, and the use of alternate hands. Sometimes, when starting to use alternate hands, the child will pass the brick from hand to hand instead of placing it straight into the container. You will need to return to guiding the child's hands to help them to move the right hand across the mid-body line over to the left-hand side of the body, and the left hand over to the right-hand side. This helps them to experience their body as a whole rather than as two separate halves.

Simple picking up and placing needs to continue until the child puts effort into reaching in all directions, working quickly and continuously, and beginning to reach for the next object immediately after placing the one before. It may require a great deal of practice before they use both hands and both sides of the body spontaneously in an integrated way.

EXTENDED PLACING ACTIVITY

One of the things that characterizes young children is the amount of energy they seem to have and how active they are. In fact, the story goes that an athlete was asked to do everything a baby did for one whole day – he lasted two hours. In contrast, some delayed children move very little in proportion to the size of their bodies. There are a number of ways in which the Placing activity can be extended to help develop this whole body movement. If you put a container of wooden bricks at one end of the room and an empty container at the other end, the child then has to pick up each brick and move across the room to place it. You can use low steps so that the child has to climb the steps each time to place a brick. You can extend this even further to an 'obstacle course' – finding a way around furniture, crawling under a chair, climbing over a box, stepping onto a small chair. For many children, these will be unfamiliar body movements, and they may not at first be able to follow a sequence of actions. You will need to help them as much as possible, taking their hand to guide them round, helping them to move their bodies and, of course, staying with them to ensure that they are always safe.

5.7 INTERMEDIATE PLACING

Once simple Placing with large objects and containers is established, you can begin to use other more complex materials requiring different and more refined movements.

RINGS ON STICKS

Placing a variety of rings on sticks provides opportunities for development of hand–eye coordination.

- Start with one stick and rings on the table in front of the child, with a small tray to one side.

- Help the child to hold the stick with one hand to steady it if necessary, and guide the child's other hand to take one ring at a time off the stick and place it on the tray, as shown in Figure 5. Taking off one ring at a time increases effort, encouraging continuity and introducing a one-to-one correspondence.

- If the child tries to take off more than one ring, you can help them to use one hand to hold down all but one of the rings each

FIGURE 5 INTERMEDIATE PLACING WITH RINGS ON STICK.

time, while guiding the other hand to take off just one ring from the top.

■ You can then help the child to put the rings back on the stick. Position the tray with the rings on so that the child has to stretch to reach them, and help the child to pick up one ring at a time.

■ You can also vary the activity by spreading the rings all over the table, then either guide the child's hand if necessary to pick up each ring, or point to each ring in turn to be placed on the stick.

You can use two or three sticks of different heights and thicknesses, and rings of different kinds. You can give the child all the rings in a container or on a tray, or you can spread them out on the table. You can put the sticks close together or spread out. There are many opportunities for the child to make chance discoveries, for example finding that there is no room on a stick for more rings, or that some rings do not fit on the thicker sticks. The child may put certain rings together, understanding that they are the same – this is the beginning of Sorting (see Chapter 10).

▨ SMALL BRICKS AND CONTAINER

Children with poor muscle tone may not have developed differentiated use of their fingers, particularly finger and thumb to pick up objects; some use the palms of the hands to do the picking up. Actively practising simple movements that bring the finger and thumb in opposition facilitates this normal movement. You need some small bricks of about 1–1.5 cm square and a container with a small opening such as a milk or juice bottle.

- Spread a quantity of small bricks on the table.

- Use a bottle with an opening just large enough to take one brick at a time, so that the child has to concentrate on looking in order to place the brick inside. Put it on the table just within the child's reach. It is possible to use a sturdy glass bottle, but only if you can be sure that it is safe to do so; if you have any doubts, it is better to use a plastic bottle.

- Guide the child's hand to pick up one brick at a time, using a finger–thumb pincer movement, and place it in the bottle.

- The child's other hand rests on the table, rather than down on their lap. If necessary, the child can use this other hand to steady the bottle, but you need to make sure the child does not move the bottle nearer to them. The effort of reaching and stretching helps the child to focus and is important for the development of these movements.

- Tip out the bricks and spread them over the table again, repeating the task with the other hand, then using both hands alternately.

- Change the position of the container – directly in front of the child, further away, to one side, to the other side, slightly above the table – to help the child practise moving their body in different directions while looking at the same time.

- Once the child is consistently able to pick up and place the bricks using the finger–thumb movement, there is no need to continue to guide the child's hands, as you can see in Figure 6.

▨ ADDITIONAL ACTIVITIES FOR DEVELOPING FINGER–THUMB OPPOSITION

TONGS

Following on from the Placing activity with small bricks, the child can use small tongs to pick up the bricks one at a time and place them in the container.

SCREWING/UNSCREWING

You can have a selection of small jars with screw-top lids to help the child practise screwing and unscrewing movements with both hands. Initially, you will

FIGURE 6 INTERMEDIATE PLACING WITH SMALL BRICKS AND BOTTLE.

need to hold and guide the child's hands so that they can feel the movement as the lid comes off or goes on the jar. Large wooden screws which fit easily into the child's hand are also excellent for learning to turn the screw in the hole.

PEGS

If you have a supply of clothes pegs and a small plastic bowl, you can help the child to hold the bowl with one hand, using the other hand to squeeze the peg between finger and thumb to open it and clip it onto the edge of the bowl. Then each peg can be taken off the bowl using the same pincer movement. You can also get pegboards with holes for putting in plastic or wooden pegs of different sizes.

BEAD THREADING

Bead threading is another Placing activity with endless variations – using different sizes of beads or things other than beads, for example rings or something with more than one hole; different 'threads', for example shoelace, cord, rope; and various 'needles', wooden or metal. You can make a curved thread by gluing it into a bent shape. With the child holding the thread in one hand and a bead in the other, they can thread from left to right and right to left. All of these intermediate Placing activities are designed to help develop fine coordination and differentiated finger–thumb movement. This will become important later on when the child begins to use a crayon or pencil.

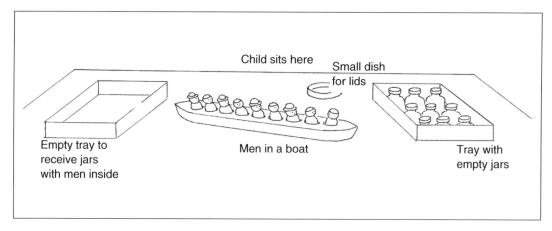

FIGURE 7 MATURE PLACING WITH MEN IN BOAT.

5.8 MATURE PLACING

Mature Placing builds on and consolidates the integrated body movement the child has already begun to develop through a wide range of Placing activities. The sequential nature of the picking up and placing becomes important.

MEN IN BOAT

For this activity, use a wooden boat with nine men and a set of nine small screw-top jars. An alternative is a base with wooden cylinders. Many children find holding and screwing difficult, but you can help them to practise using the screwing/unscrewing activities described in 5.7, Intermediate Placing. If you have any concerns about safety, then it is better to use sturdy plastic jars rather than glass ones. It is preferable to have clear plastic, as it is helpful for the child to have the added cue of seeing which jars have the men in.

- Put the boat with the men in it on the table in front of the child, just within reach.

- Put a tray with the jars on the table to the left of the child, an empty tray to the right and a small dish nearby for the lids, as shown in Figure 7.

- The child picks up the jar from the left-hand tray with both hands, placing it on the table.

- Holding the jar with the left hand, the child unscrews the lid with the right hand, placing it on the small dish.

- The child picks up a man from the boat with the right hand, placing it in the jar, and then picks up the lid using the right hand, placing it on the jar and screwing it shut.

- Using both hands again, the child places the jar on the right-hand tray.

- The child carries on until all the men are in jars.

- This is a continuous activity and the whole sequence is now reversed, the child working from right to left.

- Picking up the jar with both hands and putting it on the table, the child holds the jar with the right hand while unscrewing the lid with the left, placing it in the dish.

- The child pours the man from the jar into the palm of the open left hand and then places the man in the boat. Sometimes the child places the men in the boat sequentially, sometimes randomly; both are useful learning experiences.

- Using the left hand, the child picks up the lid to screw it back on the jar, and then holds the jar with both hands to place it on the left-hand tray.

- The child continues with the activity until the boat has been filled and the empty jars are back on the tray where they started.

This series of actions needs to be done slowly and carefully so that none of the steps is missed. Eventually, the child will be able to carry out the whole activity independently, but until then you will need to guide the child's hands whenever necessary. Although this Placing activity does involve a sequence of steps, this is not the primary focus, but the men in the boat will also be a useful piece of equipment for Sequencing activities (see simple Sequencing, in 11.5).

OBSTRUCTION PLACING

This different way of extending the Placing often appeals to children. You can use pieces of a simple puzzle board, wooden men in a boat or other similar objects, together with zip bags or purses, small tins with lids that come off easily, boxes with lids and any other suitable containers. You can prepare the activity beforehand, putting each piece of puzzle, or other object, into a container and putting all these containers into a large bowl or bucket. When you are ready to use it, put the bowl of containers on the table to one side of the child or on a chair beside the child. Put an empty container – a bowl, bucket or tray – on the other side of the table, for the empty bags and tins. Put the puzzle board in front of the child on the table. The child picks up a bag or tin from the bowl, opening it and taking out the piece of puzzle, placing it in a hole on the puzzle board, as seen in Figure 8. After each container is closed again, it is put back in the bowl on the opposite side of the table. The activity continues until all the pieces have been put in the puzzle board, and the empty bags and tins are all in a container. The process can be reversed until each piece of the puzzle has been returned to a bag or tin.

FIGURE 8 OBSTRUCTION PLACING WITH A PUZZLE BOARD.

You can introduce a variation by having more than one child involved in the activity. One child can place the pieces of puzzle in bags or tins, which the other child can then place in a bowl. One of the children can then remove each piece of puzzle from a bag or tin and give it to the other child to fit into the puzzle board.

PLACING WITH TOOLS

There is a whole range of Placing activities that involve the use of a hand-held tool. The child can use tongs to pick up bricks from the floor, putting them into a bowl or bucket. A variation is to use something like a flat food turner or fish slice to pick up and place beanbags. Another example is using a spoon to put things like beans, conkers or small bricks into a container, and for spooning them out of a jug or bowl. Children usually enjoy these activities, taking pleasure in the challenge.

5.9 PLACING IN EVERYDAY LIFE

Once children begin to pick up and place things in the Functional Learning sessions, parents can help them to participate in many of the daily activities at home. In the bedroom, they can help to make the bed, placing sheets, blankets and duvets; they can put their clothes in drawers or cupboards; they can begin to dress and undress themselves, with help at first, placing arms in armholes, legs in trousers, head in jumper, feet in socks/shoes, or buttons in buttonholes. In the bathroom, they can place toothpaste on the toothbrush, a towel on the rail, or dirty clothes in the clothes bin. At mealtimes, they can place dishes and cutlery on the table, water in a jug or glass, food on plates, dirty dishes in the sink or dishwasher. They can help with shopping, placing food in the trolley, taking it out and placing it at the checkout. They can also help with washing clothes, placing clothes in the machine or sink, on a washing line to dry or in a dryer, and placing clean clothes in cupboards and drawers. In the garden, they can place earth in pots, seeds in the earth, and water in the watering can. Once they find they can do these things, children really enjoy taking part.

The Piling Tool

CONTENTS

- What is Piling?

- Piling and Placing compared

- Piling and children with developmental delay

- Materials used for Piling

- Piling activity

- Piling in everyday life

6.1 WHAT IS PILING?

Piling involves picking up and placing a variety of objects in a continuous way to make a 'pile' or heap. This is the way children make discoveries about the properties of objects – weight, size, texture, mobility, mass, vertical and horizontal planes, the relationship of objects to each other and to the child moving them. Because it is moving, the same pile or mixture of objects constantly changes and demonstrates these different properties.

Piling continues to be a generally useful tool in everyday life. Even as an adult there are problems to solve which need a grasp of mass, like packing a suitcase. Filling a supermarket trolley, even deciding whether the amount of shopping you are going to do requires a basket or a trolley, and knowing that fragile things have to go on the top, are all related to Piling.

PILING IN NORMAL CHILD DEVELOPMENT

Piling, like Placing, is a fundamental part of the child's early exploration of the environment. Young children explore the world around them in a variety of ways continuously throughout the day. Some of these activities could be called piling, for example bringing toys and piling them on the adult's lap; pulling things out of a cupboard and piling them up on the floor; gathering together all the cushions in a room; children piling themselves on top of one another in rough play and then extracting themselves from the heap. In fact, children need to have some idea of the properties of objects before they can become skilful at using such materials as sand and water, for example filling a bottle, pouring from one large container into smaller ones, working out what will balance and what will roll away.

6.2 PILING AND PLACING COMPARED

Placing involves dealing with one object at a time, while in Piling the child is managing a variety of objects at the same time. When Placing, movement from one place to another is the most important part of the activity rather than exploring the objects, but for Piling it is the exploration of objects and their properties through activity that is important. Placing produces a more or less predictable result, but the material used for Piling means a greater degree of unpredictability which the child has to learn to tolerate; it also provides more opportunities for developing spatial awareness. There is a regularity of movement involved in Placing, whereas Piling produces irregular movements and a need for continual repositioning, an ever-changing situation. Placing could lead to a stereotyped way of dealing with material – 'patterning' – whereas Piling precludes patterning because it needs a degree of spontaneity, with the child prepared to let things happen.

6.3 PILING AND CHILDREN WITH DEVELOPMENTAL DELAY

Children with developmental delay tend either to repetitively build a tower of bricks or to chain them, placing them in a line. They rarely spontaneously seem to make the step that allows for greater variety in brick play. Or if they do, a rigid pattern emerges of the same brick pile being reproduced over and over again.

The Piling activity carried out in a Functional Learning session gives these children experience in moving objects randomly and tolerating the unexpected, which leads to less rigidity. The pile of objects by its very nature is unpredictable, encouraging spontaneity. This is very important for children with developmental delay who often prefer to keep things the same because it makes them feel safe; exploring new ways of doing things and making changes can raise their anxiety and fear of failure.

6.4 MATERIALS USED FOR PILING

The basic equipment is a large container such as a cardboard box or a laundry basket. If possible, it is a good idea to have two or three different kinds of containers available filled ready with materials. If containers or space are in short supply, variety can still be introduced by simply changing to a different container from time to time.

The container needs to be filled with objects of different sizes, shapes, textures, weights, colours, etc. They can be actual objects, such as wooden bricks, plastic bowls or cups or cartons, tin mugs, metal saucepans, cardboard plates, egg boxes or other boxes; or parts of objects, such as polystyrene packaging, lids from jars, cardboard rolls, or small sticks. The CD illustration shows a selection of material that could be used.

6.5 PILING ACTIVITY

This Piling activity can be done sitting at a table, but it can be done more energetically if the child is standing (see Figure 9). If the child has not had

FIGURE 9 A CHILD PILING.

experience of Piling before, or if this is a particular problem area, you can work behind the child, moving their arms. The movement needs to be vigorous and effortful. You can continue to help the child to move the materials around until they can carry on in a continuous way unaided.

The objects are taken out of the container and put onto the table one by one; they are then moved around for some time until being replaced in the container. The movements involved need to be fluid and rhythmic. There is no set time limit or real ending to this activity. It is the actual movement of the objects that is important rather than the placing, making it an ever-changing experience. You can add to the unpredictability of the activity by joining in, moving the materials around along with the child.

A different effect can be achieved by using a table of a different size, height or shape, for example a round table, or even a chair. As with Placing activities, the container can be placed in a different spatial relationship to the child, for example on a chair to the child's left, on the floor to the child's right, under the table or behind the child.

Putting things back into the container is an important part of the activity. As the child becomes more aware of the objects being manipulated and their properties, they get better at putting a mass of irregular objects into a defined space. How the child does in this part of the task is probably a good guide to his understanding as a whole. This can be done as a group activity where each child has to tolerate what may be seen as the 'interference' of others.

6.6 PILING IN EVERYDAY LIFE

Once children begin Piling in the learning sessions, the activity can be extended to the everyday environment. Children can be helped to pile toys into a toy box, to pile clothes into the washing machine, and to take the clothes out of the washing machine and pile them in a laundry basket. Out in the garden, they can help to fill up a wheelbarrow or bucket with sand, leaves or grass. All of these activities provide opportunities for learning by doing, exploring the environment in as many different ways as possible, and developing fluid, free-flowing, rhythmic body movement.

The Banging Tool and the Drawing Tool

CONTENTS

♦ What is Banging?

♦ Banging and children with developmental delay

♦ Materials used for Banging

♦ Introducing Banging activities

♦ Scraping – an extension of Banging

♦ Drawing

♦ Banging and drawing in everyday life

7.1 WHAT IS BANGING?

Banging is associated with the development of the hands in the very young child, and eventually leads to rhythmic movement of the whole body using both hands. It is the basis of the child's ability to grasp, hold and make use of a tool – tool here meaning an implement, not to be confused with the Learning Tools which are mental or cognitive tools.

DEVELOPMENT OF BANGING

Development of hand function in the baby depends not only on the motor control of shoulder, arms and hands but also on visual, perceptual and cognitive development. The earliest hand movements of the newborn are involuntary but, from birth to three months, as the hands begin to open, they become more intentional. By five months, the baby is deliberately reaching out and grasping objects in both hands. The clutching or grasping is not yet very controlled, and the baby's jerky movements bring objects into contact with each other, often making chance noises. Gradually, grasping and holding objects comes increasingly under control until, at about nine months, the baby intentionally brings one object into contact with another or with a surface, an obvious example being banging on the table with a spoon. The continuity of holding and banging objects together is the basis for the development of the Banging Tool.

Young children progress to using tools such as sticks or wooden hammers to bang with, getting a great deal of pleasure from banging rhythmically on different surfaces. They use both hands and both sides of the body, their movements becoming strong and energetic as they explore the surrounding space. Of course they are interested in the sound, but they are also looking at what they are doing as they focus their attention on the sticks or other tool. Eventually, spoon and sticks give way to pencil and crayons for drawing and making permanent marks on paper and, later on, symbols leading to the development of writing. Children usually become very excited when they see their own mark-making and often want to share their delight, with comments such as 'Look what I've made'.

7.2 BANGING AND CHILDREN WITH DEVELOPMENTAL DELAY

Delayed children not only have many problems in motor development, but they have a poor body image because of their limited motor experiences. Their motor control is not well developed and they are slow to use their hands to explore the environment around them. They are often reluctant to make marks on paper, being anxious or afraid of failing to produce what might be expected. To help bring about better coordination, they need prolonged practice of simple energetic movements in which the different parts of the body begin to work together. You can use Banging activities in the Functional Learning sessions to help facilitate this integrated movement. These activities also help children who do not have a well-developed grip and find it difficult to use hand-held tools such as a spoon.

7.3 MATERIALS USED FOR BANGING

 Much of the simple material used for Banging activities can be found around the home – the CD shows some of the things you can use. Targets for Banging can include chairs, tables, boxes and xylophones. The large wooden bricks used for picking up and placing can now be used for banging. Different sizes and thicknesses of sticks, wooden spoons and wooden hammers can also be introduced. Drums, metal tins and other sturdy containers can be used as targets. Banging can even be done with bells, as well as chains of different colours, sizes, thickness and weight which many children enjoy. If a child is very sensitive to sound, you can cover the table top with pillows or cushions.

7.4 INTRODUCING BANGING ACTIVITIES

The aim of Banging activities is to combine the use of a tool with as wide a range of body movements as possible, focusing the child's attention and facilitating body integration. The movements can be varied, slow or fast, involving both hands independently and together.

WOODEN BRICKS

- You can start with wooden bricks, choosing a size to fit the child's hand, with small bricks for small hands and larger bricks for larger hands.

- Sitting behind the child, help the child to hold a brick in each hand.

- Guide the child's hands to bang the bricks together rhythmically. Banging objects together like this is also related to Pairing (see 8.1), illustrating the interdependence of the Learning Tools.

- Next, make banging movements all over the table.

- You can extend the child's movements in all directions by banging other parts of the table such as sides and legs. You can even bang the legs of the child's chair and your chair so that the child bends and stretches, gaining more body awareness in doing so.

STICKS FOR BANGING

- Change the bricks to sticks. Start by helping the child to use a stick in one hand, then change the stick to the other hand and, finally, give the child two sticks, one in each hand.

- Just like the bricks, guide the child's hands to bang the sticks all over the surface of the table, as well as table and chair legs, stretching and moving in all directions.

- Even if you need to cover the table with cushions to dampen the noise, it is still important to encourage large, flexible movements, until you can feel the child begin to take over, banging independently for a short time, as shown in Figure 10.

- As you continue to extend all the banging movements, help the child to move energetically, stretching out their arms and repeating different patterns of movement.

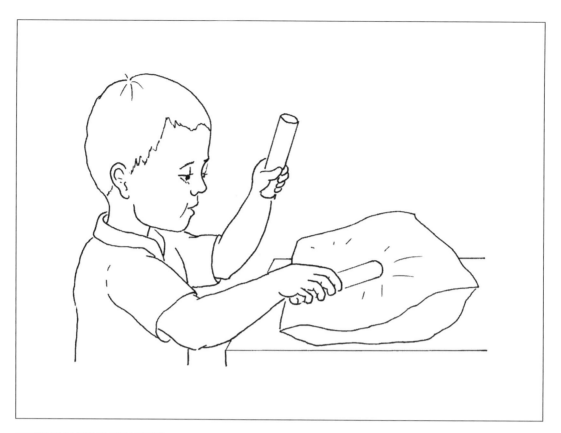

FIGURE 10 BANGING WITH STICKS.

USING TARGETS

- Use the sticks with a drum or tin as a target, holding it above the table so that the child has to look up and bang more vigorously. Move the target around and hold it at different heights, as the child bangs with a stick in one hand, shown in Figure 11, and then both hands. Sometimes the child will need the help of your guiding hands and, at other times, can do the banging independently for short periods.

- You can use a different target, and again the child does the banging with one stick then changes to two sticks.

- If you use a drum and tin or metal lid together, you can guide the child's hands to bang with the sticks to make different sounds and rhythms, sometimes with one hand, sometimes with two hands together, sometimes alternating hands, banging on one target or moving from one target to the other, in as many variations as you can think of.

- You may need to work with a helper, so that one person can hold and move the target while the other helps the child.

FIGURE 11 BANGING USING A TIN AS A TARGET.

It may be a long time before the child can do this banging by themselves with sustained effort, and you will need to give ongoing support until you find the child taking over and doing the banging independently. The video on the CD shows Christopher being helped by his father, until he can begin to enjoy banging with the sticks himself.

CHAINS

Lengths of metal chain, which can be bought from hardware shops, can provide additional variations for Banging activities. You may need to guide the child's hands at first to make sure that they are safe when using the chains.

- The chains can be light or heavy, they are flexible to hold and make interesting noises, either by chance or when intentionally banging one chain against another or on different surfaces.

- You can encourage the child to use both hands, with a chain in each hand.

- You can also put the chains in containers, and help the child to explore different sounds when banging them together, or on surfaces like chairs, table or floor.

All of these banging experiences encourage very energetic, effortful and variable movement. As they become increasingly pleasurable, eventually they also become intentional, independent, self-motivated activities.

7.5 SCRAPING – AN EXTENSION OF BANGING

The sticks that have been used for Banging can also be used for Scraping – a transition between Banging and drawing activities:

- Help the child to hold the sticks firmly to make large continuous scraping movements across the surface of the table – horizontally from left to right and right to left, vertically and diagonally, away from themselves and towards themselves. You can also make circular movements, clockwise and anticlockwise.

- Just like the banging, guide the child's hands, using one hand, then the other hand, then both hands together and both hands alternating.

- Vary the speed and size of the scraping movements shown in Figure 12, to give the child as much experience as possible.

7.6 DRAWING

The Banging and Scraping activities can naturally lead on to early drawing, and the sticks are replaced with crayons. There may be children who are not quite ready to move straight into drawing, or who may be hesitant about the change to making marks on paper. If so, you can introduce an intermediate activity using a sand tray, helping the child to make marks in the sand tray with a stick, using similar movements to the scraping.

MATERIALS FOR DRAWING

You will need plenty of sheets of strong white paper to cover the whole table for the initial drawing activity, keeping the paper in place with clamps or tape. You can use rolls of old wrapping paper or wallpaper, cut into sheets. You will need smaller sheets of paper for later drawing work. Start off with thick, sturdy crayons that will easily fit into the child's hand. Eventually, you can give the child things like pencils, brushes or chalk to draw with. The whole experience changes if, instead of working on the table, you use a board and easel with brushes and paint – for example, the paint can run and the child has to cope with unexpected results.

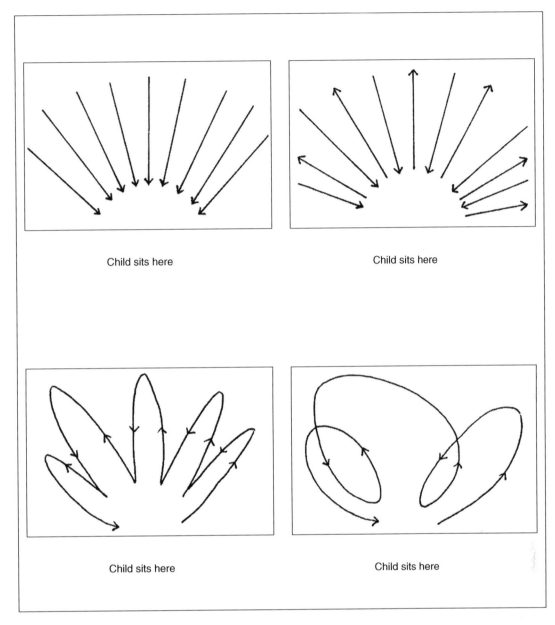

Child sits here

Child sits here

Child sits here

Child sits here

FIGURE 12 SCRAPING MOVEMENTS DONE WITH STICKS.

■ LONG-ARM DRAWING

In this activity the child uses a crayon to make rhythmic patterns over the whole surface of the paper.

- ■ Help the child to hold the crayon firmly between thumb and fingers, using one hand to start with. Guide the child's hand to move horizontally, vertically, diagonally and in a circular motion – the same as scraping – covering the paper with continuous marks that flow across the page.

- Change the crayon to the other hand, continuing to move in all directions across the paper.

- Help the child to hold a crayon in each hand, making patterns on the paper using the different movements, moving both hands together in the same direction or different directions, or alternating one hand then the other.

- Vary the pace, intensity and size of the movements, giving the child lots of practice.

- You can gradually move your hands away as you feel the child beginning to explore for themselves, using the crayons to create their own patterns, freely and with enjoyment.

Some children find this continuous movement difficult and seem to be fearful of making marks on paper. These are new experiences and they dislike the unfamiliarity. They may withdraw their arms or let the crayon drop from their hands. There are various strategies you can use to help them until they are able to find their own pleasure in using this Learning Tool. You could, for example, keep the paper on the table but return to scraping with sticks, then move back to trying a crayon again, moving between these activities until the child feels less agitated. You could return to banging, but using a crayon on paper. You could guide the child's hands to make the patterns of movement in the air, gradually moving down to the table and then up in the air and back to the table. Once the child is settled, you could try this with the child holding a crayon and with some paper on the table. If you have access to a large sand tray, you could help the child to use their pointing finger to make the patterns in the sand, covering them over each time so that the marks disappear.

JOINING THE DOTS

Once the child can control the crayon and move it across the paper with ease, there are many other drawing activities they can try. One of these is joining the dots to help hand–eye coordination:

- Make two large dots on the paper a few centimetres apart.

- Start by guiding the child's hands, placing the pointing finger of one hand on one of the dots, while using the pointing finger of the other hand to draw an invisible line from one dot to the other, moving back and forth several times between the dots, as shown in Figure 13.

- Then give the child a crayon and, still keeping the child's pointing finger on one of the dots, guide the child's hand to draw a line from this dot to the other one.

- Vary the position of the dots, placing them vertically, horizontally or diagonally on the paper. Help the child to use their finger to trace the proposed line each time and then join the dots with the crayon.

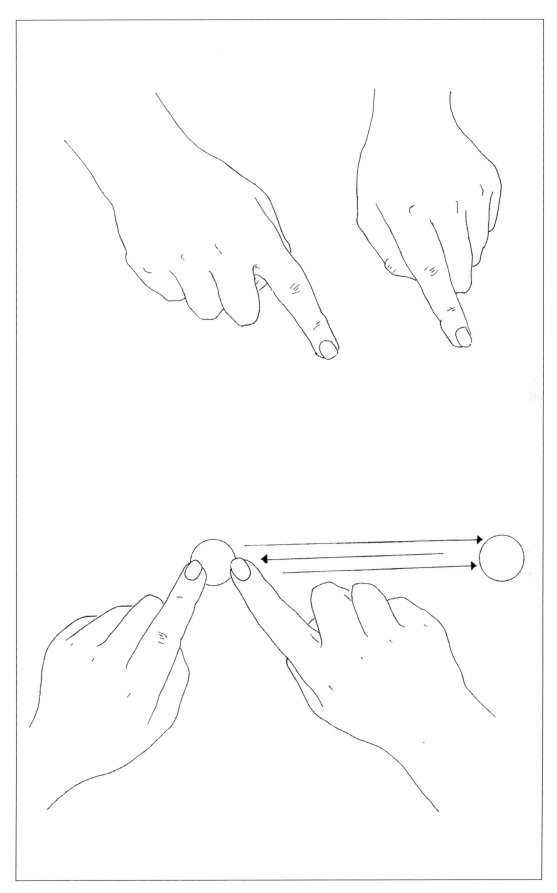

FIGURE 13 DRAWING – JOINING THE DOTS.

- You can help the child to draw a square using the same method, making one line at a time with two dots for each line, joining up each set of dots in turn until they make a square.

- Eventually, you will find the child can join up all four dots themselves to make the square.

- You can also help the child to make a triangle using three lines instead of four.

Spatial awareness and the ability to draw lines between dots can be used in problem-solving games on specially designed worksheets, for example linking objects by drawing a line (see Chapter 13 and examples of worksheets on the CD).

7.7 BANGING AND DRAWING IN EVERYDAY LIFE

Once Banging and Drawing have been introduced in the Functional Learning sessions, parents can begin to help the child with developmental delay to participate in some of the activities commonly enjoyed by young children. There are various banging toys available, for example a hammer toy with pegs for banging into holes, a xylophone or a drum. The child can be helped to use these toys at first, until they can play with them spontaneously. As they become more competent, some children may be able to have their own small hammer to bang nails into wood, with a parent always available to help and, most importantly, to make sure the child is safe. As an extension of banging with sticks, they can begin to use tools in the kitchen, helping to beat, mix and cut. Parents can help the child to use crayons for scribbling and eventually more controlled colouring-in, other common activities which young children like to do.

The Pairing Tool

CONTENTS

- What is Pairing?

- The pointing finger

- Materials used for Pairing

- Introducing Pairing

- Simple Pairing

- Intermediate Pairing

- Mature Pairing

- Extension of Pairing into everyday activities

8.1 WHAT IS PAIRING?

Pairing is putting together two objects that are the same. Developmentally, it is possible to see the genesis of pairing overlapping with Placing and involuntary Banging as early as six months. When exploring and playing, the baby may, for example, pick up and hold an object in either hand and then, first by chance and then deliberately, bang them together. Later at about nine to ten months, when picking up becomes increasingly competent and intentional, the baby may pick up a well-known object like a shoe and then look around to find the other shoe.

Studies have shown that babies are aware of faces and can distinguish between pictures of faces and other pictures. Faces have symmetry, for example there are two eyes, two eyebrows, two cheeks, two ears. Later the child becomes aware of other body parts that are also pairs – legs, arms, hands, feet, fingers, and toes. A good deal of playful, pleasurable interaction takes place between child and parents/carers when the child points to different parts of the body and the adult names them.

8.2 THE POINTING FINGER

NORMAL DEVELOPMENT

The child's ability to point and follow visually along a row or line of objects or cards is important to the development of the Pairing Tool and then the Matching Tool. Eventually, pointing becomes a useful learning strategy in activities such as Sequencing, Coding, Intersectional Sorting and Worksheets (see Chapter 13) and in more traditional educational subjects like reading, writing and number work. In normal development, the use of the pointing finger appears during the second part of the first year. It is one of the earliest pre-verbal gestures. The child points away from the body using the index finger, trying to touch objects out of reach and to show parents/carers what they do or do not want. Pointing is also concerned with self-awareness, with children pointing to themselves and using their name or the personal pronouns I, me and mine.

THE CHILD WITH DEVELOPMENTAL DELAY

In children with developmental delay, the pointing finger may appear very much later and may not be readily available for learning. There are a number of strategies to help facilitate both children's awareness and use of the pointing finger:

- Initially, you need to help the child to recognize that one finger is separate from the others. With activities where the child needs to point, you can hold your hand over the child's hand, leaving the pointing finger free.

- Sometimes you have to stretch out the child's pointing finger, to keep it straight rather than remaining soft and curled, helping the child become aware that this is a very special finger, perhaps by gently touching it.

- You can find something the child enjoys playing with, placing it together with a small biscuit where the child can see both. Help the child to point to one of them which you then give to the child.

- The child can be helped to use this pointing gesture in the course of daily activities.

- You can use some of the simple picking up and placing activities to help the child practise pointing. If you put rings on the table, you can help the child to point to a ring, pick it up and place it on the stick. You can spread bricks on the table and then help the child to point to a brick each time before placing it in a container.

8.3 MATERIALS USED FOR PAIRING

PAIRING OBJECTS

To introduce simple Pairing, it is a good idea to use bricks or beanbags which the child is already familiar with from Placing activities. In addition, you need to collect a large assortment of pairs of other common everyday objects found in the home and the outside environment. Each pair of objects needs to be identical. They must also be things that cannot be broken, can easily be picked up and held in the child's hands, and can immediately be recognized. Some examples are: metal or plastic knives, forks, spoons; metal or plastic biscuit-making shapes; small tins or other containers; wood or metal egg cups; wooden napkin rings; small metal or wooden doorknobs; wood or metal rings; keys. Many other ideas are illustrated on the CD. You will need two or more trays, preferably without pictures or patterns which might confuse or distract the child, and large enough to hold 12 bricks or up to 10 pairs of other objects.

PAIRING CARDS

Once the child is Pairing objects competently, cards can be introduced. They can be simple line drawings to start with – pairs of simple shapes such as circle, square or triangle; pairs of simple objects such as ball, house, tree, car or cup. For both the shapes and the drawn objects, each pair needs to be identical. The CD shows a few examples. As the child progresses, cards with more complex pictures can be used, for example identical pairs of people, animals, flowers, fruit or vegetables.

PAIRING/MATCHING BOARD

The board designed for use in Pairing and, later on, for Matching activities is made of hardboard approximately 35 cm long x 15 cm wide. A strip of thin dowelling across the middle of the board divides it into top and bottom spaces. The spaces are outlined with dowelling to keep objects and cards in place.

8.4 INTRODUCING PAIRING

Pairing will be described as a progression of activities, not as fixed stages which every child must pass through. Not all children will necessarily progress through all the activities in the same way. Some children will take months on the very simplest Pairing of bricks. Other children will be able to start with the Pairing board and very soon move on to finding pairs from among many objects. It is knowledge and understanding of the individual child that will help determine the appropriate progression of activities for that child. Flexibility of approach is all-important, and always being prepared to change back to an earlier activity if the child becomes anxious and uncertain.

8.5 SIMPLE PAIRING

Initial Pairing with objects will flow more easily if two people can work together, one to present the materials while the other sits behind the child guiding the child's hands, as you can see Christopher's parents doing on the CD video. To begin with, the identical wooden bricks that have already been used for Placing are used for Pairing.

- An empty tray is placed on one side of the table, leaving space in the centre of the table in front of the child.

- The person helping stands to one side of the table with a tray of bricks, placing a pair of bricks on the table in front of the child.

- The person guiding helps the child to pick up both bricks simultaneously and then place them together on the empty tray.

- Continue helping the child to move pairs of bricks from table to tray as smoothly and rhythmically as possible.

- When the target tray is full, the person helping removes it, replacing it with an empty tray, this time on the other side of the table.

- The Pairing is repeated, with the person helping again placing the pairs of bricks on the table, while the person who is guiding helps the child to pick up and place them simultaneously on the tray.

- The child needs to work energetically, with effort, reaching out as far as possible and using both sides of the body.

- This simple Pairing is practised until the person who is guiding begins to feel the child reaching out spontaneously to pick up a pair of bricks from the table and place them on the tray.

- Even when this happens, there may still be times when the child needs a guiding hand again for a short time.

- Constant adjustment in response to the child's cues enables the child to work confidently and with pleasure, becoming more competent all the time. You can see this happening with Christopher on the CD video.

- For variety, this simple Pairing activity can also be done with identical pairs of beanbags.

Children who have settled in to the rhythm of Pairing things like bricks and beanbags – picking up the pairs themselves some of the time, using both hands and looking, as shown in Figure 14 – can be introduced to pairs of common objects.

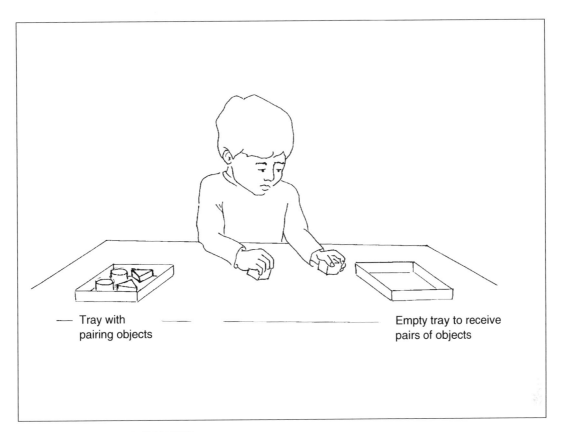

Tray with
pairing objects

Empty tray to receive
pairs of objects

FIGURE 14 SIMPLE PAIRING WITH BRICKS.

- Put two trays on the table, one on each side, leaving a clear space in front of the child. The tray on the left is empty, and the one on the right contains three pairs of identical objects, for example two bricks, two eggcups or two keys.

- To start with, put a pair of bricks on the table in front of the child and guide the child's hands towards them.

- The child picks up both bricks simultaneously, one in each hand, and places them on the left-hand tray.

- Put another pair of objects – the eggcups – on the table in front of the child who reaches out, picks up both eggcups and places them on the left-hand tray.

- Finally, do the some thing with the last pair of objects.

- Repeat the process but take the objects from the left-hand tray this time and the child will put the pairs of objects on the right-hand tray.

- If the child hesitates, unsure which tray to put the pairs on, you can tap the appropriate tray or guide the child's hands.

- When the adult feels the child is ready, the objects can be changed to three different pairs, using the pairing process just described.

Some children become very attracted to a particular object, continually handling it and interrupting the continuity of the Pairing. If this happens, it can be changed for a different pair of objects. Some children return to simple Placing, picking up the objects and putting them on the tray one at a time. Other children try to pick up both objects in one hand. If this happens, you can return to guiding the child's hands until they get back into the rhythm of Pairing. It is important that the child picks up each pair of objects simultaneously, one in each hand, placing them together on the tray. This not only encourages maximum effort and the use of both hands, but it helps to increase the understanding that these are separate objects that make up a pair.

When the child is settled and working confidently, you can gradually increase the number of pairs being used, first to four pairs then up to six pairs. The next change would be increasing the number of pairs placed in front of the child each time, first two pairs then three pairs, which means finding each pair from among more objects. You can help the child by picking up one object and holding it next to the identical object on the table, and then guiding the child's hand to pick it up from the table and put it in your hand. Put the pair of objects to one side so that the child has fewer to choose from next time. But as the child's understanding increases, you can return the objects to the table each time, so that there is always the same number of objects to choose from. Each change will be a new challenge, so you will need to facilitate the child as much as possible, in order to make it a successful and pleasurable experience.

8.6 INTERMEDIATE PAIRING

Once the child has become familiar with pairs of common objects, developing some understanding of Pairing and the ability to work independently some of the time, the Pairing board can be used. This will be quite a new experience and may need to be introduced very gradually.

Put the board on the table in front of the child. To start with, six pairs of identical objects are used which the child is already familiar with from earlier Pairing, for example two small bricks, two buttons, two rings, two small boxes, two cotton reels and two bottle tops. They need to be of a suitable size to fit in the spaces on the board. To facilitate the child in the early stages of this new activity, it is a good idea for the pairs of objects to be very clearly different from each other, for example a pair of bricks and a pair of rings rather than a pair of large bricks and a pair of small bricks.

- Put one object on the top left-hand space on the board and the identical object on the table just below it.
- Help the child to use the pointing finger of the left hand to point to the object on the board and then to the empty space below.

- While keeping the child's left pointing finger on the object on the board, help the child to pick up the other object from the table and place it in the empty space.

- It may be necessary to help the child to focus on the pair of objects by using the pointing finger to point to the one in the top space, then the one in the bottom space.

- Continue with the pairing, working along the board.

- Once all the objects are in pairs, they are taken off the board and the process is repeated from right to left.

- Some children may need to be helped with this early Pairing on the board for some time. For variation, some of the pairs of objects can be changed from time to time.

The next change in intermediate Pairing is introduced when appropriate for the individual child. This time use six pairs of identical objects. Set out one of each pair in the top spaces on the board, and place the others on the table, each one directly below its pair. Help the child to pair the objects, following the same process used for the initial Pairing on the board, working in both directions for spatial and perceptual practice. The objects along the top of the board can be changed around occasionally, to extend the problem solving. As the child begins to anticipate where to place each object with the identical one, you can gradually withdraw your guiding hands so that the child can work alone, but always being ready to return to helping the child if necessary. Every child has a unique pace of working, and some children may take longer than anticipated before being able to work independently for any length of time.

As the child becomes more competent, the objects for pairing are put farther away from the board.

- Set out one of each pair of objects on the board.

- Put the other one of each pair in a group on the table, to one side of the board.

- The child selects an object from the group, taking it along the objects on the board, finding the identical object and putting it in the space below.

- Some children may need a guiding hand to help them do this. It can also be a help to use the pointing finger to locate the identical object on the board and the space to put it in.

8.7 MATURE PAIRING

By now, the child has had a great deal of practice with Pairing activities, and can work with objects and the Pairing board with effort, continuity and enjoyment.

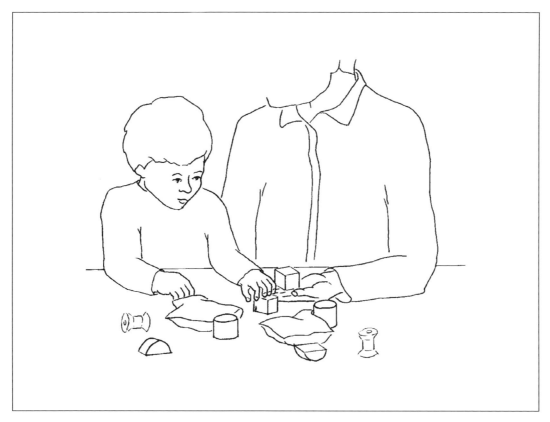

FIGURE 15 MATURE PAIRING WITH OBJECTS SPREAD ON THE TABLE.

Pairing can be extended even further by spreading objects all over the table so that they are no longer in pairs but mixed up. Six pairs are used to begin with, but more are added as the child becomes more experienced.

■ Pick up one object, placing it in the palm of your hand, and hold this hand, with the object visible, next to the identical one on the table.

■ Help the child to pick up the object from the table and place this one in your hand as well.

■ Put the objects back on the table, so that the number of objects the child has to choose from remains the same.

■ Repeat this pairing process until the child becomes increasingly at ease with this activity.

■ You can change some of the pairs, continuing until the child begins to anticipate the next move by reaching out to pick up and pair the object in the adult's hand without any prompting, as Figure 15 shows.

The activity now becomes a pleasurable game and can be extended further.

■ Again, pairs of objects are spread all over the table, starting with six pairs and gradually adding more.

- Pick up one object, holding it so that the child can see it, but this time not directly next to the identical one on the table.

- The child now has to scan all the objects on the table, looking for the identical one before placing it in your hand.

- Put the two objects back on the table, mixed in with the others, so there is always the same number of objects on the table.

- The object the child has to find can be held in different positions – sometimes to one side, sometimes the other, sometimes in front, high up and low down, to encourage the child to keep looking and moving in different directions, reaching and stretching.

- Eventually, the child will be able to do the pairing more or less independently, finding each pair and putting it on a tray, as Helen does on the CD video.

PAIRING WITH CARDS

For the child who is able to pair objects freely and easily, Pairing cards can be introduced, using sets of cards with simple line drawings at first, then moving on to more complex images. Just as with object Pairing, each pair of cards has identical images, as shown in Figure 16.

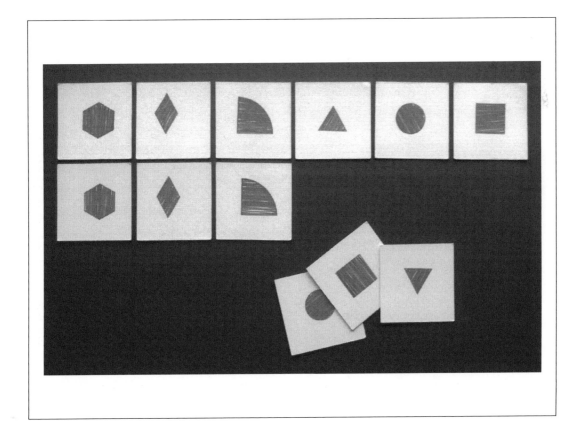

FIGURE 16 PAIRING CARDS.

- To start with, the procedure is the same as simple Pairing with objects. Put a tray to one side of the table for the child to place the cards on.

- Put a pair of cards on the table in front of the child, then help the child to pick them up together and put them on the tray.

- Continue to give the child pairs of cards to be picked up and put on the tray, helping where necessary, but with the aim of encouraging the child to work alone as much as possible.

- As with object Pairing, once the child has put all the pairs of cards on the tray, they are removed, the empty tray is put on the other side of the table and the card Pairing is repeated.

- As soon as the child has become familiar with Pairing cards, they can be used on the Pairing board just like intermediate and mature Pairing with objects. You can eventually progress to the activity where the cards are spread all over the table, also following the same process used with objects.

8.8 EXTENSION OF PAIRING INTO EVERYDAY ACTIVITIES

When the Pairing Tool is well established, commercially produced card games can be used, such as Pelmanism or Find the Pair. There are various ways of doing this – this is just one example. The cards are spread out over the table, turned face down. The child picks up one card, turns it over and holds it in their hand, then turns over the other cards on the table until the pair is found. The child puts the pair of cards to one side. The other cards are turned face down on the table again and the game continues until all the pairs are found. This Pairing can be played as a family game with everyone taking turns to find the pairs of cards. Pairing can also be linked to body image, and the child can participate with growing understanding in nursery rhymes, naming different parts of the body that are in pairs. Once this level of competence in pairing is reached, the child can easily move on to Matching with objects and cards.

The Matching Tool

9.1 WHAT IS MATCHING?

Matching is defined as resembling or corresponding in some essential respect, according to the Oxford Dictionary (*The Concise Oxford Dictionary of Current English*, 1995). The mental tool for Matching allows the child to compare and contrast one object or image with another. The child keeps an object or image in mind – the model – and then searches for one that seems the least different from the model.

In everyday life, if we are in a room that we have not been in before and we are looking for the door to leave by, chances are we would not open all the cupboards and wardrobes, but we would look around the room for the door that looks the least different from – or the most like – the door we have as a model in our mind. Another example would be looking for a particular book that we remember being a certain size and colour. We would probably not look among books of a vastly different size or colour from our 'model' book, but we would tend to focus on books that looked more like the book we had in mind.

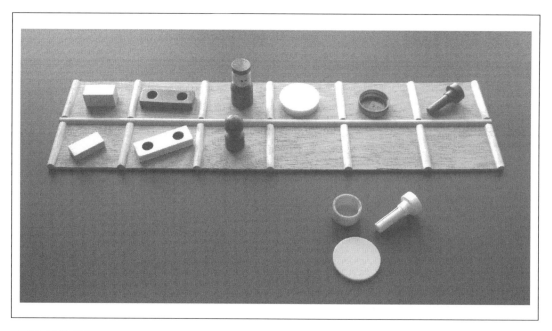

FIGURE 17 SIMPLE MATCHING WITH OBJECTS ON A BOARD.

9.2 MATERIALS USED FOR MATCHING

MATCHING BOARD

For simple Matching, the board is the same as the one used for Pairing (see 8.4). For intermediate and mature Matching, the board is the same width but 46 cm or more in length. Several boards can be used together for mature Matching, to increase effort and understanding.

OBJECTS FOR MATCHING

Objects are used for the earliest simple Matching on the Matching board. Although Matching is about the way things correspond, it is also about differences. To begin with, in the Matching activities, there are only small differences between objects, for example two wooden circles of slightly different sizes, two rings of different materials, two buttons of the same size but different colour, two shells of the same kind but slightly different size, two clothes pegs of the same type but different material (and see Figure 17). As the activity progresses, the differences become more complex, for example two different types of shells, two keys of different shapes, two buttons of different size and shape, or two different types of screws.

MATCHING CARDS

It is important to keep increasing the variety of work. As the child progresses, cards can be used to extend the range of ideas, instead of objects which have practical limitations. Specially made cards for intermediate and mature Matching activities are designed to introduce finer discriminations and more complex concepts, such as matching by association – hat and coat, umbrella and rain, knife and fork, tree and leaves, arm and sleeve. The CD gives examples of both objects and cards for Matching.

9.3 INTRODUCING MATCHING

Matching depends on a firm foundation of Placing and Pairing. It requires a certain degree of development of perceptual and spatial ability. It also helps if the child can point and visually follow along a row or line. 'In matching, the important moments of learning are not those when the [child] finds the match … *The learning is in the searching* – it is this ability to scan, discriminate and reject' (Brooks, no date).

The point has already been made in 2.3 that the Learning Tools are not distinct entities but often merge or overlap. This is perhaps especially so with Pairing and Matching which are very much interdependent. They have been dealt with in separate chapters simply for ease of description.

With very young developmentally delayed children and older children who are severely delayed, their Learning Tools may only just be emerging. They will need to follow the progression through the various Pairing activities described in Chapter 8, which may take some time, before they can move into Matching. For other less delayed children, it will be possible to introduce Matching early on in the Functional Learning programme. But it may still be necessary to spend time helping them use their pointing finger, as illustrated in Figure 18. Also, for all children, if they are showing anxiety or uncertainty when Matching, it is always possible to change to a developmentally earlier Pairing activity, to help reduce the anxiety and consolidate their learning before trying Matching again.

9.4 SIMPLE MATCHING

MATCHING WITH OBJECTS

For those children who have been progressing through Pairing activities, working with increasing self-motivation and understanding, it can still be a big step to move into Matching and they may be working at the edge of their competence. When simple Matching activities are first introduced, it may be necessary to move back and forth between mature Pairing activities and Matching to reduce any anxiety the child may have. It cannot be stressed enough that the aim of Functional Learning is for the child to be successful. The adult needs to be flexible, finding different ways of facilitating the child to minimize failure, and to fully extend the child's effort, repetition, continuity, understanding and pleasure in this work.

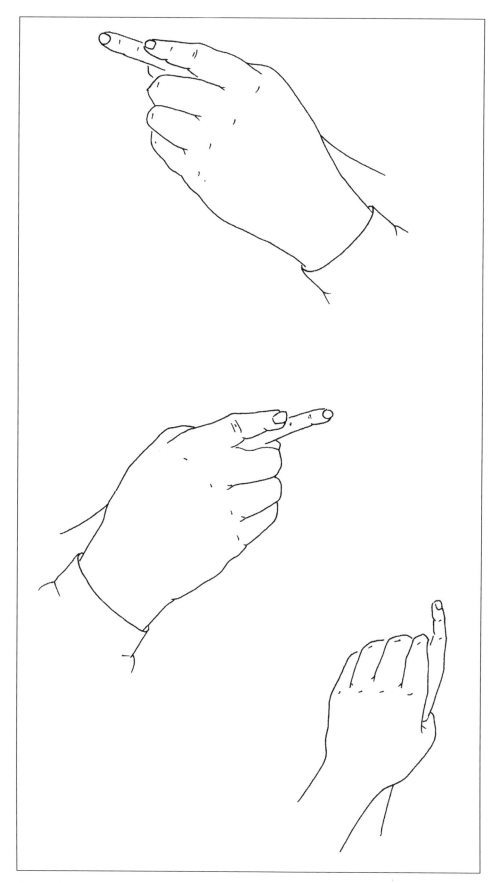

FIGURE 18 USING THE POINTING FINGER.

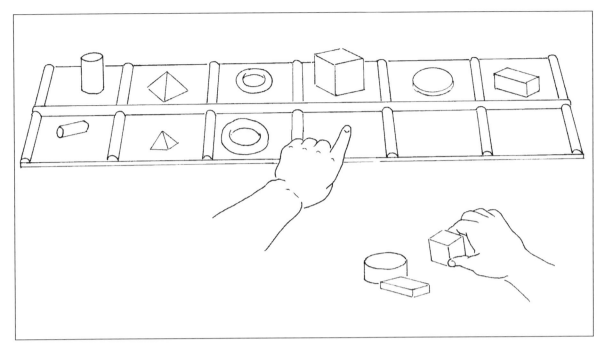

FIGURE 19 SIMPLE MATCHING USING THE POINTING FINGER.

Simple Matching starts with the same board used for intermediate Pairing and six pairs of non-identical objects, where there are only small differences between the objects in each pair.

- Put the Matching board on the table in front of the child, with one of each pair of objects set out along the top spaces.

- Place the other six objects in a small group on the table, just to the right of the board.

- Starting with the first object on the left – the model – help the child to point to it, to choose from the group of objects on the table the one that is the least different from the model, and then to place it in the space on the board under the model.

- The child works in sequence along the row of objects as shown in Figure 19, using the same procedure of pointing to the object (the model) each time, keeping the model in mind and finding the match, until all the matching objects have been placed on the board.

- You can then repeat this procedure, with a change of direction, working along the row of objects on the board, this time from right to left.

Sometimes the child may be pointing to one object, but may pick up a different object and put it on the board with its partner. If this happens, you can guide the child's hands to help them focus on the object they are pointing to, for

FIGURE 20 MATCHING BOARD IN DIFFERENT POSITIONS.

example by lightly tapping the child's pointing finger on the object, and then to find the one that matches it. Other possible strategies are pointing to the matching object on the table, or moving it slightly away from the other objects and nearer the board, so it becomes obvious to the child which one it is.

You can introduce variations, to help the child scan in all directions and get practice in discriminating differences. Only small changes are made at first, for example, using the same objects but changing their positions on the board, and helping the child to work along the board, sometimes using the left hand to point to the model and sometimes the right. As the child becomes more confident, you can change the objects regularly.

MATCHING WITH CARDS

You can use cards for simple Matching. Initially, the items on the cards will show only small differences. For example, they can be simple drawn shapes where one of each pair is solid and the other is an outline. Cards are presented on the Matching board, using a similar procedure to object Matching described above, with variations introduced when the child becomes ready for them. If the child has been Matching with objects and then cards are introduced, even though cards have been used for Pairing, the child may show some anxiety at the change. You need to be aware of this and help reduce the child's anxiety, perhaps by reducing the number of cards, or returning to object Matching, or even using a mixture of pairs of cards and objects.

9.5 INTERMEDIATE MATCHING

As the child's Matching ability begins to develop, the objects and cards used have greater differences and require finer discriminations. The method of presenting the material described for simple Matching is still used, and the child needs the pointing finger to follow along the board and to help keep the model in mind, while searching for an object or a card that is the least different. You can use a longer board, with spaces for eight pairs of objects or cards, and eventually you can use two boards together, placed end to end. You can use the board in different positions, so that it is sometimes vertical, sometimes horizontal, sometimes diagonal, as Figure 20 shows. You can move the group of objects or cards on the table further away from the end of the Matching board and put them in different places – sometimes on the left of the board, sometimes on the right, above or below the board.

9.6 MATURE MATCHING

Cards used for mature Matching are designed with increasingly complex images. You can introduce this new material using just one Matching board for either six or eight pairs of cards. You can set out one of each pair of cards on the board as usual and place the other cards at an increasing distance from the boards, on the table top to begin with, then on the floor and eventually even outside the room.

- Keep the Matching board on the table with one of each pair of cards in the spaces along the top of the board. Scatter the other cards on the floor.

- The child starts at one end of the board using the pointing finger to identify the first card at the top and then, keeping the model in mind, moves away to find the match among the cards scattered on the floor.

- Sometimes the child forgets which card is needed, and has to return to the Matching boards to point again to the model to recall which card to look for.

- The child works sequentially along the board, looking for each Matching card in turn.

Eventually, you can extend the activity by placing the cards outside the room. This implies the child is able to move away and still feel confident. An additional variation is to give the child more cards than there are spaces on the board. With experience, the child realizes that these extra cards are not needed and can be rejected.

9.7 EXTENSION OF MATCHING ACTIVITIES

Children who have developed the Matching Tool can begin to join in other pleasurable activities at home and in the classroom. There are simple workbooks and worksheets with prepared line drawings, offering a range of problems that include opportunities for Matching. For example, the child has to point to an object and look for the match, or use a pencil to draw a line joining matching objects, which may be things that go together, such as cup with saucer, flower with vase, shoe and sock, or spoon and fork.

10

The Sorting Tool

CONTENTS

- What is Sorting?
- Links with Pairing and Matching
- Materials used for Sorting
- Seeding
- Separating
- Simple Sorting
- Intermediate Sorting
- Mature Sorting
- The use of language in Sorting activities
- Sorting in everyday life

10.1 WHAT IS SORTING?

The mental tool for Sorting is vital in helping children to sort out and make sense of the world around them. Babies have an innate capacity to sort out their personal world from the time they are born. For example, it has been found that babies distinguish pictures of adult faces from other pictures, and they turn their heads towards their own mother's milk and away from milk pads from different mothers. Sorting is characterized by flexibility of response and the making of choices. It is the basis for classification – recognizing that objects can be the same or similar and can be grouped together in sets. It depends on the child having a firm foundation of Placing, Pairing and Matching.

10.2 LINKS WITH PAIRING AND MATCHING

There is a strong link between Sorting and Pairing and Matching. In Pairing, the child brings together things that are the same. When the child progresses to Matching, things are being compared in terms of differences. These elements of identical – Pairing – and least different – Matching – are the ground work for Separating (see 10.5 below) and Sorting. In Separating, the child is creating a set of things that are identical. When Sorting, the things that make up the set need not be identical, which immediately opens up a whole range of criteria possibilities for forming a set – material, colour, weight, size, use, place of use, age, gender. This clearly demands a flexibility of thinking that the child has already begun to experience in Matching. This is a huge move forward from the safety of content and method experienced in Pairing and Separating.

10.3 MATERIALS USED FOR SORTING

OBJECTS FOR SORTING

For the early simple Sorting activities, you can help to make links with previous Functional Learning activities by using some of the objects that have already become familiar to the child when Pairing and Matching. But you will also need to have a broad range of other materials available for Sorting, to give the child as much experience as possible. Things from around the house are ideal, for example bottle tops, buttons, combs, brushes, clothes pegs, small jars, wooden spoons, tins, cups, chains, batteries, cotton reels, corks, small brushes, beads, small bags or keys. You can also use things from the outside environment, such as pine cones, small stones, shells, small flower pots, tools, balls or conkers. Some collections of objects will be identical, for example bricks all the same or spoons all the same. Some will be similar, like keys or bottle tops. By having many different kinds of objects, and at least 20 or more of each object, you can provide the child with the opportunity to make up a great variety of sets. It also gives plenty of scope for sorting using different criteria. The CD illustrates the great wealth of interesting and appealing material that you can collect and have available.

CONTAINERS FOR SORTING OBJECTS

You will need some containers for the child to put objects into when sorting. They should be relatively sturdy, and of a size that will allow up to six containers to fit on the table as the child progresses. Small plastic, flat-bottomed dishes with sides can be used, or any other similar container that is available that will keep the objects from tipping out onto the table. They store easily if all the same size, and are less distracting if all the same (neutral) colour. It is also useful to have some plastic trays to put the objects on when giving them to the child for sorting. Having two different kinds of containers can be of help to children who are new to Sorting, providing extra cues, to distinguish the mixture of objects to be sorted from the objects sorted into sets, as Figure 21 shows.

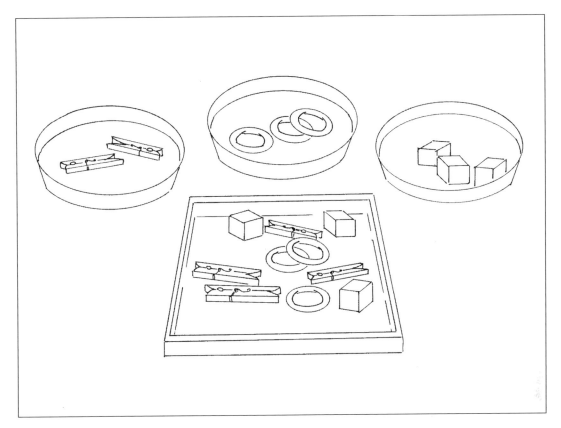

FIGURE 21 SORTING TRAY AND DISHES.

SORTING BOARDS

The special boards used for Sorting with cards are made of hardboard, each one 30 cm x 30 cm in size, with a thin strip of wood forming a rim around the outside, to keep the cards in place on the board. As Figure 22 shows, each board is divided into 9 squares of 6 cm x 6 cm, with thin dowelling to outline the squares, making a clear space for each card. It is useful to have a number of boards, as card Sorting usually starts with two boards, increasing to four, and then six or more, so that the child's effort and understanding are constantly being extended.

SORTING CARDS

In addition to objects for Sorting, you will need a large collection of cards to use on Sorting boards. You can make the cards using sturdy white card that cannot easily be bent or torn. Each card is 5 cm square, to fit the spaces on the Sorting boards. Each set has at least nine cards, for the nine spaces on a board.

A practical advantage of using cards is that they are relatively easy to handle, move around and store. Using cards gives the child a wider experience of more abstract ideas and concepts. Just like objects, various criteria for sorting can be applied to the cards. The amount of information on the cards can be varied so

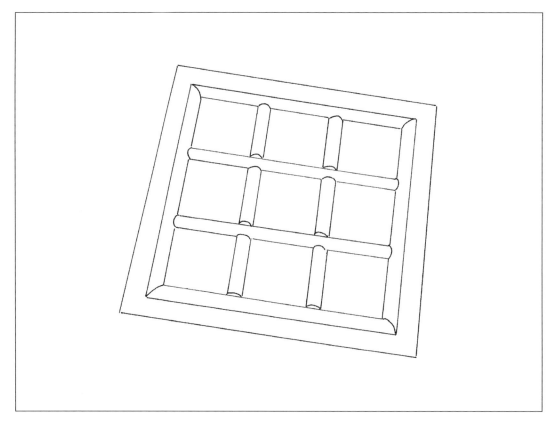

FIGURE 22 SORTING BOARD.

that, for example, the image can be distorted or only partly visible or show only part of the whole.

For simple Sorting, you can start with line drawings or cut-out pictures of identical objects, for example nine balls, nine trees, nine houses. For intermediate Sorting, the cards contain more information, for example nine different cars, nine kinds of fruit, nine different keys. Mature Sorting begins to move into concept sorting, for example different kinds of transport – car, train, ship, plane, bus, bicycle, taxi, helicopter, truck – or different places where people live – cottage, block of flats, castle, igloo, large house, row of houses, tent, bungalow, straw hut. Other cards for mature Sorting show parts of the whole object, such as different parts of a car. You can always extend and add to the sets of cards to suit the needs of the children you are working with. The CD illustrates a variety of different ideas for sets of Sorting cards.

During the initial Sorting activities, you will need to organize the cards to keep everything safe and minimize any confusion, by putting the cards on the table ready for sorting and taking them off again, ready for the next activity once the child has sorted them onto the boards. Children often want to handle and take control of the cards themselves when the adult is setting up the boards or changing the cards at the end of the activity. This is usually a defence against anxiety and fear of failure. If it happens, you can just settle the child by asking them to wait and helping them to put their hands down on their lap.

10.4 SEEDING

Seeding is a way of providing the child with information when doing the Sorting activities by putting one or more objects in a dish or cards on a board. This acts as a model for the child when sorting the rest of the material. During early Sorting activities and if children are particularly anxious and uncertain, all but one or two objects or cards might be seeded so that the child only has to place a few items to begin with.

10.5 SEPARATING

Separating is a way of sorting by continuously choosing objects from the same set rather than picking up objects at random; it is more like pairing. Some children become very persistent and insistent on doing it this way, rather than picking up the first object that comes to hand, then scanning the dishes to find the set it belongs with. It is a less demanding and 'safer' way of working. What we are really looking for is a flexibility of thinking that can use both separating and random sorting appropriately. There are various ways you can help a child to become more flexible and spontaneous in making choices. One way of doing it is to cover the objects with your hand, leaving only a few visible for the child to select from, and changing the position of your hand so that there is a different mixture of objects for the child to choose from each time. You could put just a few mixed objects on the tray and, when the child has sorted these, add a few more, and so on, or you could give the child the objects one at a time.

10.6 SIMPLE SORTING

▨ INTRODUCING SIMPLE SORTING WITH OBJECTS

Start with two sets of familiar identical objects that have been used in previous activities, such as clothes pegs and bricks.

- Put a small tray on the table in front of the child and two dishes, positioned towards the top of the table, so that the child has to stretch to reach them but can see their contents.

- Seed both dishes, with several bricks in one and pegs in the other, as shown in Figure 23, making sure that the child is watching while you do this.

- Place one brick on the tray and then point to the dish containing the brick.

- The child may pick up the brick and put it in the dish with the other bricks, but you may need to guide the child's hand to do this.

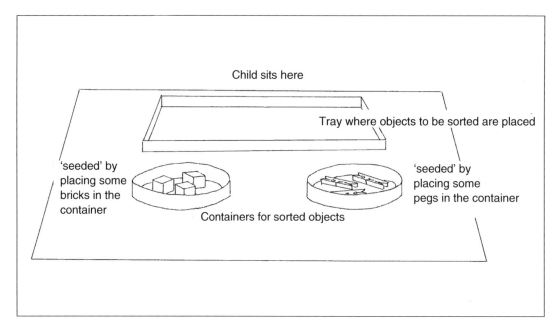

Child sits here

Tray where objects to be sorted are placed

'seeded' by placing some bricks in the container

'seeded' by placing some pegs in the container

Containers for sorted objects

FIGURE 23 SIMPLE SORTING WITH SOME OBJECTS SEEDED.

- Next, place a peg on the tray and point to the dish containing the pegs.

- If necessary, help the child to put it in the dish with the other pegs.

- Some children will look at the dish, by eye-glide, but may not pick up the object and put it in. You can respond to the eye-glide, which is a way of communicating, by guiding the child's hand.

- Continue with the activity until all the bricks and pegs have been sorted into the two dishes. With the last few, it may not be necessary to point to the dishes, if the child is beginning to understand what to do and can do it without the prompt. If the child mixes up the objects, perhaps putting a brick in with the pegs, simply return it to the tray and point to the bricks, helping the child to put the brick into the appropriate dish if necessary.

You can repeat this simple Sorting several times more, keeping the same objects but changing the position of the dishes each time – one on either side of the child, both dishes on one side, then on the other side. Seed the dishes and continue to give the child just one object at a time. If the child is settled and working well, you can gradually introduce different sets of identical objects, just changing one set each time, for example keeping the bricks and changing the pegs for buttons.

CONTINUATION OF SIMPLE SORTING WITH OBJECTS

Once the child becomes familiar with this early Sorting, you can begin to work with more sets:

- Start by extending the Sorting activity to three sets of identical objects.

- Seed the dishes with two or three of each object.

- Gradually increase the amount of material on the tray from one object to several, doing it in such a way that the child is not worried by too much material.

- You may need to continue to point to the appropriate dish each time until the child begins to anticipate where to put the object.

- Continue until the child has sorted all three sets.

- You can repeat the sorting of these sets several more times, changing the position of the containers and adding more material, until the child begins to sort with only minimal help.

- You can change the sets, still using identical objects, keeping the original two, the clothes pegs and bricks and adding a third, for instance spoons.

- Continue introducing other sets like this, building up the child's Sorting ability.

These are guidelines for introducing simple Sorting with a child who has been Placing, Pairing and Matching, but who is still in the early stages of acquiring the Learning Tools. They have been worked out over a long period of clinical practice, with many different children with developmental delay over a wide age range, from three years to 12 years, and with a wide spectrum of difficulties. But within these guidelines, the way of presenting the materials and carrying out the activity can be flexible – adjusted and adapted to suit the needs of the children.

Early Sorting has been described using a particular way of setting out containers and working through a gradual process of introducing the activities. Delayed children can have spatial problems, their fine motor coordination is often poorly developed, and they sometimes have difficulty focusing on relevant information. Some very sensitive children become agitated when objects roll or fall, and they can become overwhelmed and distracted by large quantities of material. For these children in particular, using containers can help overcome these difficulties, making the objects more manageable as well as defining the working space. But, of course, there are other children who can handle quantities of material, and for them there may be occasions when they sort into piles on the table, without any containers. Also, for example, in the initial simple Sorting activity, one brick or peg at a time is being given to the child using a tray; but some children would be able to manage without a tray, and you could simply put the brick or peg on the table. There are many different options according to the children you are working with.

CARD SORTING

For children who have been working with simple object Sorting activities, and who show understanding of sorting up to three sets with some independence, Sorting with cards can be introduced. Some children make the change to cards and boards quite easily. For other children, it needs to be a very gradual process and, as a transition, it may help to sort simple cards into dishes before moving on to boards.

INTRODUCING SORTING BOARDS

To introduce the Sorting boards, for children who find change difficult, you may need to start by making a link with the earlier Sorting using objects:

- Put a Sorting board on the table and a dish of nine familiar identical objects, for instance nine buttons. Guide the child's hand to pick up one at a time and place it in a square on the board.

- Do this with other objects until the child is freely putting objects on the board.

- You can now begin to introduce card Sorting activities.

INTRODUCTION OF SORTING CARDS

You can follow the same kind of gradual process to introduce Sorting cards as you do with objects:

- Start with one set of cards, for example identical balls, and one board.

- Put one card face down on the table in front of the child.

- The child picks up the card, turns it over, looks at the picture and places the card in one of the squares on the board. Repeat with the rest of the cards, helping the child as much as necessary.

- Cards are presented face down as a way of helping the child to focus on the picture once the card is turned over, before looking at the boards to choose where to put the card. But there are times when the cards may be presented face up, in order to reduce any anxiety the child may have about this new activity.

- Once the child is familiar with placing the cards on one Sorting board, then add a second board and use two sets of simple Sorting cards, keeping the balls and adding a set of identical coloured stripes. Seed several cards on each board.

- Present the cards one at a time, alternating the cards from the two sets, and continuing until all the spaces on the boards have been filled.

- You may need to guide the child's hand to choose which board the card goes on or you can point to the appropriate board. If the child puts a ball with the stripes, you can simply give it back and help the child to put it on the appropriate board.

You can gradually introduce variations. For example, you could keep the same two sets that you have been working with but change the position of the boards. You can reduce the number of seeded cards as the child becomes more confident. You can keep one set of cards but change the other set to a different one. You can also try giving the child a small pile of two or three cards, but still making sure only one card at a time is picked up. If the child becomes anxious, which they may show by pushing the cards away or turning all the cards face up, return to offering one at a time, waiting until the child has settled before trying again with two and then three cards. Once the child is enjoying sorting two sets of simple cards and eagerly anticipating more each time, then add another board and use three sets of cards. For those children who can manage it, the whole pile of two or three sets of cards is presented at once, shuffled so that they appear in a mixed order. Of course, any change such as a new set of cards or an extra board needs to be introduced in such a way as to minimize the child's anxiety. It is important for the child to be successful and not to become hesitant or afraid of failure.

10.7 INTERMEDIATE SORTING

For intermediate Sorting, there is a gradual introduction of increasingly complex objects which are similar but non-identical. Some children will need to be helped to make the change very gradually, following a similar process as the simple Sorting. To start with, you could use one set of identical objects that the child is already familiar with, such as clothes pegs, together with a set of similar, but non-identical objects, such as keys. Other children will be ready to go straight on to sets of non-identical objects, starting with two sets, for example keys and bottle tops, and going on to three or more. Use as many helping strategies as necessary – seeding, guiding the child's hand, pointing to the relevant container – until the child begins to work increasingly independently.

Sorting cards can also gradually be increased in complexity, for example sets of circles or triangles of different sizes, as shown in Figure 24. The child can then move into concept sorting, for example sets of things where the items within each set are different, like dogs, flowers, fruit, trees, houses, shoes, shells. You may not need to seed the boards for children who are very competent with cards. You will find that experienced children begin to anticipate where the empty spaces are as the boards begin to fill up, and they are able to change the cards from one board to another once it becomes clearer what the sets are. This is the kind of flexible sorting that helps to develop problem-solving ability.

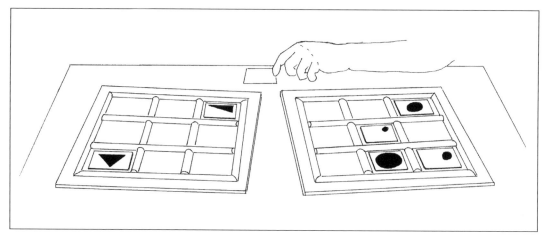

FIGURE 24 INTERMEDIATE SORTING WITH CARDS.

10.8 MATURE SORTING

Mature Sorting begins to move into categories of things, such as transport, furniture, clothing, things used in the kitchen, things found at the seaside, and eventually sets of parts of a whole, such as parts of a car, parts of a house, parts of a face. Objects and cards can be sorted by material, colour, size, weight or use. Each object or card can fit into several of these criteria, so things can be looked at from various perspectives. The child can be asked to change the criteria by which materials are sorted. For example, objects can be sorted into sets of spoons or pegs and then sorted by material; or pegs can be sorted first by material and then by colour.

Children can become very creative in the use of the Sorting Tool, and may choose to sort into quite different sets from those you may have had in mind. It will eventually become possible to extend object Sorting by giving the child several dishes and a large tray of mixed objects. The child makes choices about how to use the containers and decides how to sort the objects into sets. Something similar can also be done with cards.

10.9 THE USE OF LANGUAGE IN SORTING ACTIVITIES

The initial introduction to simple Sorting does not require the use of language, apart from a few words when setting up Sorting boards or removing cards, for example, 'hands down' or 'wait'. But once the child is competent in Sorting, language can be added so that the session includes simple communication and understanding simple directions.

When the cards have been sorted onto the boards, you can ask the child to pick up certain ones, for example, 'give me all the cards with houses'; 'give me all the people'; 'give me two houses and two men'; 'give me a boy, a house and a chair'. This does need a certain level of understanding, but again you can use the pointing finger or the guiding hand to help the child with this new experience. A variation is for the child to ask you for cards, for example, 'I want all the houses'; 'I want the house and the boy', etc. With increased competence, there are many possible ways of using the cards for listening and talking.

10.10 SORTING IN EVERYDAY LIFE

Once the Sorting Tool is established, there are many different activities that children can begin to take part in and enjoy, practising and extending their new-found ability. In the home environment, Sorting can very quickly be built into activities such as sorting the family wash, sorting their own clothes from the rest of the family clothes, sorting the cutlery, sorting the shopping into different cupboards, or sorting their toys. When they are outside, children can be helped to collect things like stones or pine cones, or shells on the beach. Many other possibilities will arise naturally out of everyday activities.

11

The Sequencing Tool

CONTENTS

♦ What is Sequencing?

♦ Sequencing and children with developmental delay

♦ Using the pointing finger

♦ Materials used for Sequencing

♦ Simple Sequencing

♦ Intermediate Sequencing

♦ Mature Sequencing

♦ Sequencing in everyday life

11.1 WHAT IS SEQUENCING?

Sequencing is a complex form of thinking that has a linear element. It is a series of 'events' that take place one after another. Sequencing can also involve rhythm, as in clapping hands or walking. When we clap hands, the sequence is made by the regular bringing together of our two hands, but when we stop clapping, there is no trace of the sequence. You can also make a sequence with objects placed one after another in a line, and they do leave a trace so that you can see the sequence that has been made. It is the linear element that enables us to repeat the sequence forwards or backwards, or to fill in any gaps in the sequence. For other sequences like cooking or getting dressed, we need to understand the various elements that make up the sequence. In dressing, for example, we need to understand what shoes, socks and trousers are, in order to know in what order to put them on. So Sequencing can involve Sorting and has elements of Placing, Pairing and Matching. It also requires spatial awareness which can be developed through Brick Building. The child needs experience of the activities to develop these Learning Tools before Sequencing is introduced.

11.2 SEQUENCING AND CHILDREN WITH ■■■■ DEVELOPMENTAL DELAY

As young infants grow and develop, moving about and exploring their environment, they develop the ability to plan and sequence their actions. They can put together a series of movements to accomplish something, so when babies see a toy they want, they will crawl over to it, reach out and pick it up (Greenspan and Wieder, 1998). Young children's early Sequencing ability is often taken for granted. They are able to carry out quite complex sequences of motor actions that can be both rhythmic and continuous – babies follow parents with their eyes and, later on, children clap hands, walk, run, swing arms and climb.

But children with developmental delay, whose movements are not yet well co-ordinated, have difficulty carrying out a sequence of actions. They may have difficulty carrying out even a one-step sequence, such as opening a door to get something they want. They have problems doing things like clapping hands or placing objects in a continuous sequence. Without this basic sequencing ability, delayed children are unable to follow a sequence of ideas and therefore unable to understand what happens next. Their world is full of uncertainty, reinforcing their desire to keep everything the same. Many of the Placing activities, described in Chapter 5, provide experiences to help develop this fundamental Sequencing ability, in addition to the specific Sequencing activities described here.

11.3 USING THE POINTING FINGER

Using the pointing finger is essential for being able to follow a sequence – the child looks down the length of the arm to the pointing finger at the end, as Figure 25 shows. This is a simple way of helping to find the next place in a sequence, which is just a series of spaces forming an imaginary line. It might be a sequence of objects one after the other, for example brick, button, brick, button, etc., or a sequence of cards that might have triangles going from smallest to largest.

11.4 MATERIALS USED FOR SEQUENCING

■■■ OBJECTS FOR SEQUENCING

For the early stages of Sequencing, you need solid, plain wooden bricks, large to medium size. Because they are very stable, it is easy for the child who is just beginning Sequencing to put them in a line. It is better not to have rounded objects for these early activities, as they may roll or move about and are not so easy to place in a line.

FIGURE 25 SEQUENCING USING THE POINTING FINGER.

As the child becomes more competent, you can use other simple objects – bean-bags, rings, buttons and clothes pegs, etc. To help with sequencing objects in a line, you can have a special board made of hardboard, or similar, with strips of dowelling to make a row of single defined spaces. You can also make a block of wood with shallow holes for sequencing with round objects in later Sequencing activities. A thick string, with a large knot on the end to stop objects coming off, can be used for threading a series of objects, such as large wooden beads, small bricks with holes, wooden or plastic rings and cotton reels.

MATERIALS FOR SEQUENCING BY SIZE

Nesting boxes, stacking cups, Russian dolls and graded rings on a stick help children begin to understand a size sequence. They can also use the Montessori cylinder blocks, consisting of a solid wooden base with holes for cylinders graded in size. And you can have a collection of objects of different sizes that can be made into a size sequence, for instance spoons, jars, bricks, and plastic shapes.

SEQUENCING CARDS

You can make sets of cards to extend the Sequencing activities. Start with simple, clearly defined line drawings. For a child who can sequence two objects – brick, bean-bag, brick, beanbag, etc. – use cards with drawings of shapes, so, for example, you might have cards with squares and triangles to form a sequence of square, triangle, square, triangle, etc. You can have cards for sequencing by size, perhaps a set of six or eight cards, the first one a small square, the next a bit larger, and so on up to the largest. You can make cards to illustrate other types of sequences, for instance one that starts with an incomplete picture and ends with a complete one, perhaps a series of drawings of a car, where each card has more of the car showing until the last one is a complete car. You can also illustrate a simple story that moves through time.

 Many different examples of objects and cards for Sequencing are included on the CD.

▨ DRAWING MATERIALS

The introduction of drawing or colouring into Sequencing activities indicates progress in establishing other Learning Tools, particularly Banging, Scraping and Drawing. Once a child can use a crayon or pencil they can produce a colour sequence on paper. You need to have large sheets of paper readily available along with crayons or coloured pencils.

11.5 SIMPLE SEQUENCING

Sequencing starts with the early Placing activities, described in 5.6. Placing bricks one after another into a container using alternate hands is a sequence of actions. However, although the child can feel the movement and see the bricks going into the container, once the bricks are placed there is no visible trace of the sequence. But by placing the bricks in a line the child can see that a sequence has been made.

▨ CHAINING

For chaining – placing bricks next to each other in a line – use bricks that are all the same size so that they make a clear line.

- Set out three or four bricks in a line to one side of the table so that the child can see the direction and pattern of the sequence.

- Put additional bricks in front of the child.

- Help the child to add bricks to the chain, using alternate hands and keeping up a steady rhythm by just sliding the bricks into place in the chain.

- Help the child to make horizontal, vertical and diagonal lines of bricks – working from left to right, right to left, top to bottom, and bottom to top.

- Doing this in reverse and taking the sequence apart is as important as creating it. Each time the child makes a chain, help them to remove each brick in turn and put it back in a pile on the table, which is a sequence in itself.

■ After the child has had some practice with chaining, you can add another variation. When the chain is being taken apart, as each brick is removed, it can be used to start another chain, either going the same way or changing direction.

OTHER EARLY SEQUENCING ACTIVITIES

You can use a wooden cylinder block (see materials for Placing in 5.5) for Sequencing. The child points to a hole and puts in a cylinder, starting at one end and continuing in sequence to the other end. You can extend this activity by helping the child take the cylinders out of the block one at a time, putting them in a line on the table, as they did with the chains of bricks. The boat and boat men used for mature Placing, in 5.8, can also be used like the cylinder block for Sequencing. Other simple Sequencing activities are nesting boxes and stacking cups that can be placed one inside the other, and cotton reels for threading onto a thick thread one at a time, and then taken off the thread again one at a time.

TO SET UP A TWO-OBJECT REPEATING SEQUENCE

Practising the simple activities described will help to develop the child's understanding of sequencing. Now you can introduce making a two-object sequence:

■ Using two sets of objects, for instance bricks and rings, put some bricks on one side of the table and rings on the other side. These can be put on trays, and for some children this is necessary, but if they are just on the table they can be moved into place in the sequence more easily.

■ Set out some of the objects in front of the child to show the pattern of the sequence, for example A, B, A, B, A, B (or brick, ring, brick, ring), as shown in Figure 26.

■ The child continues the sequence, using alternate hands to place a brick and a ring in turn.

■ It can be helpful to use the special board for this activity, making it easier for the child to follow the sequence by placing the objects in the defined spaces on the board.

■ The sequence can be taken apart, sliding the bricks and rings along the table one by one in an easy, rhythmic movement, using alternate hands, putting a brick to one side and a ring to the other.

■ As a next step, to help the child understand the linear element of the sequence, you can draw a line on paper and the child puts the sequence of objects (A, B, A, B, A, B, etc.) along the line.

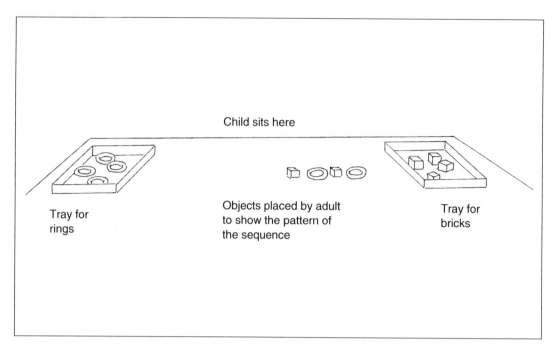

FIGURE 26 SIMPLE SEQUENCING – A REPEATING SEQUENCE WITH TWO OBJECTS.

CARDS FOR SIMPLE SEQUENCING

Finally, you can introduce cards, using them in a similar way to the objects. Using two sets of cards with simple drawn shapes, for instance squares and circles, set out a sequence of circle, square, circle, square. Place the cards in a line, edge to edge, making the sequence clear and the child adds the rest of the cards to it.

It is quite important to spend time on these early Sequencing activities, giving the child the opportunity to become very familiar with them, because going on to make a three-element sequence will be a big move forward.

11.6 INTERMEDIATE SEQUENCING

Making a sequence of three elements or objects marks the beginning of real sequential thinking without the assistance of alternate hands.

MAKING A BRIDGE BETWEEN TWO-OBJECT AND THREE-OBJECT SEQUENCES

One way of helping the child to make the huge change to a three-object sequence is to fuse or put two objects together:

- Put a small ring on a large brick (AB), and a third object, for instance a button, C, next to them. Make a line of a few more of these combinations to show the pattern of the sequence: (AB), C, (AB), C, (AB), C.

- Put a brick, a ring and a button in a small dish, helping the child to add them to the sequence. Continue adding to the sequence like this.

- You can help the child further by using the board, where the defined spaces will act as a guide for making the sequence. The child moves along the board pointing to a space and putting down the next object in the sequence.

SEQUENCING THREE ELEMENTS OR OBJECTS

By observing the child's progress with the Sequencing activities, it will help you decide when to introduce true Sequencing with three elements or objects. You will need to give the child as much support as possible, guiding their hands when necessary (see under Placing in 5.4) and helping them to use the pointing finger. You will need to be flexible and, if the child seems anxious, be prepared to adjust the materials to enable them to succeed. Always provide a trail of objects indicating the pattern of the sequence, which means the child does not have to guess what comes next but can follow the information given to them.

- Use three very different objects, for instance a brick, a clothes peg and a button. Set out a line of objects to show the pattern of the sequence: A, B, C, A, B, C (brick, peg, button, brick, peg, button).

- Place one of each of these objects in a small dish.

- Help the child to point to each object in turn along the sequence already on the table, ending up pointing to the next space in the sequence. Then guide the child's hand to pick up the next object from the dish, placing it in the sequence.

- Continue like this, helping the child to make the repeating sequence of three objects.

- Once all the objects have been placed in the sequence, they can be removed in sequence. Have three dishes, one for each object. Working from the opposite end, help the child to point to each object in turn then pick it up and put it in the appropriate dish.

It may take quite some time and a good deal of practice for the child to develop an understanding of a three-object repeating sequence, before they can begin to make it themselves. So you need to maintain the support of the guiding hand and only withdraw it very gradually. Eventually, the child will be able to make the sequences working from left to right, top to bottom and vice versa. To extend the activity further you can use three sets of cards with drawn shapes, just like you did with two sets. By this time, the child is beginning to understand that all the information needed is on the table in the form of objects or cards, indicating the pattern of the repeating sequence. You can provide other problem-solving opportunities – setting out a sequence with gaps for the child to fill in, and even creating sequences on a larger scale, on the floor, if the child feels secure with such a change.

You can begin to use some language as the child becomes more familiar with the idea of Sequencing. For example, using three objects, with one of each in a small dish, sequence two objects and ask the child to place the third object from the dish. As understanding increases, you can ask the child to add the next two objects to a three-object sequence. This introduces turn-taking which can be done later on with another child, encouraging increased flexibility and helping the child to think sequentially.

11.7 MATURE SEQUENCING

DRAWING AND COLOURING

You can introduce drawing and colouring activities into Sequencing once the child can use a pencil or crayon. This means plenty of experience in long-arm drawing, covering large sheets of paper with endless curving lines, horizontal and vertical lines, and joining up dots, using great physical effort with both left and right hand. For more detail, see 7.6.

- First, introduce a colour sequence with two colours only, for example making several small lines in a sequence on the paper, alternating one colour with the other. The child then adds lines to this colour sequence.

- Once the child has the idea of what to do, you can make a sequence with horizontal, vertical or diagonal lines, with the sequence sometimes going from right to left, sometimes left to right, and so on. You can also draw a sequence of simple shapes like circles and triangles.

- Eventually, you can move on to using a three-colour sequence as the child's competence increases.

EXPANSIVE SEQUENCING

An expansive sequence is a series that gets larger in one direction and smaller in the other. This can be introduced once the child can sort by size and shows good spatial awareness in Brick Building.

- Nesting boxes that fit inside each other have already been introduced for simple Sequencing. When the child is familiar with the different sized boxes, they can be put in a line in size order.

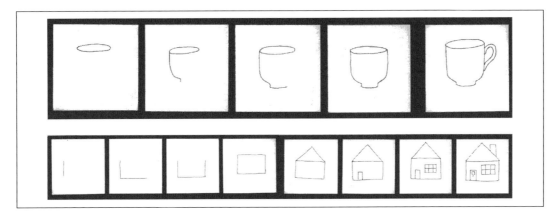

FIGURE 27 MATURE SEQUENCING – EXPANSIVE SEQUENCES.

- You can use any other objects available to give the child more experience of expansive sequences – for example, bottles, dolls, keys, cones, or rings of different sizes, for making sequences from large to small and small to large.

Cards are very useful for expansive Sequencing. With cards it is possible, for example, to show a sequence that starts with an incomplete drawing, perhaps the first few lines of a house, ending with a complete drawing of a house, as shown in Figure 27. Cards can also illustrate a sequence in which an object is moving slowly from one place to another. With size, number also comes into play and realization that, as objects are removed from one place to another, two expansive sequences are created, the one getting bigger while the other gets smaller. A simple 'story' can also be told with cards, for example you can illustrate the steps of a simple activity like making a cup of tea.

11.8 SEQUENCING IN EVERYDAY LIFE

Children can begin to participate in the many everyday activities that involve a sequence of steps or actions once they establish an ability to follow a sequence. Some of the everyday Placing activities, suggested in 5.9, can be extended if the child has an understanding of Sequencing. For example, the child may start with placing a pillow on the bed but, with more competence in Sequencing, this can be extended to making the bed completely. They can dress themselves if the clothes are laid out in the order they need to be put on. Cooking gives the child Sequencing opportunities of all kinds, from the simplest activity of stirring a pot or making toast to making a cake. Children can participate in shopping once they are able to cope with the noise and crowds of people. Buying a single item, such as a bag of sugar, offers endless possibilities for Sequencing in either a few steps or with many steps, according to the child's growing self-assurance. In all these everyday sequential activities it is clear that the Learning Tools overlap and they are used in conjunction with each other.

12

The Brick Building Tool

CONTENTS

♦ What is Brick Building?

♦ Brick Building and children with developmental delay

♦ Materials used for Brick Building

♦ Introduction to Brick Building

♦ Brick Building from a model

♦ Link with Drawing

♦ Everyday play activities related to Brick Building

12.1 WHAT IS BRICK BUILDING?

Brick Building is the experience of placing bricks in different positions and involves an understanding of spatial relationships. Young children commonly start by chaining bricks, as seen in 11.5 – placing them in a row – or building them up. As they continue experimenting, they may produce a structure by chance until, eventually, after a lot of experience, they have a structure in mind then proceed to build it. A prerequisite for Brick Building is a firm foundation in Placing, Piling, Pairing, Matching and Sorting.

The child's understanding of space has its origins in the early development of body movements. Children explore and adjust to the space around them through their early play, and through the many different body postures and positions as they move about. They begin to understand the front, back, left and right, and top and bottom of the body in relation to the surrounding space. The exploration of space is associated with praxis 'which involves the planning and sequencing of novel motor acts. It is a bridge between cognition and motor abilities and encompasses . . . the organization and execution of a response to sensory input' (Williamson and Anzalone, 2001).

12.2 BRICK BUILDING AND CHILDREN WITH DEVELOPMENTAL DELAY

Delayed children who do not have a wide range of body movement therefore have a limited understanding of space and their own position in space. Through repeated daily practice during Functional Learning sessions, their movement and consequent exploration of space begin to develop. This new learning is based on the growth and use of the Learning Tools for Placing, Piling, Pairing, Matching and Sorting in many different contexts and with a wide variety of materials. Once these children begin to notice the difference between the intention of an activity and the outcome, there is a gain in understanding and an increase in the variety of activities. With this growing foundation of understanding, together with the newfound ability to work with effort and increasing autonomy, children can be introduced to activities to facilitate the Learning Tool for Brick Building.

12.3 MATERIALS USED FOR BRICK BUILDING

You need two identical sets of wooden bricks in a variety of shapes for Brick Building and some plain trays to put the bricks on. The bricks need to be plain, not coloured, also large and stable enough to stand upright without tipping over.

Once the Brick Building is established it can be linked with drawing. You can use white card to make a set of line drawings of brick models of one, two, three or more bricks.

12.4 INTRODUCTION TO BRICK BUILDING

Sitting beside the child is the best position for Brick Building, so that the child's position in relation to the bricks is the same as yours. You need to have a tray to one side of you on the table, and so does the child, leaving a space in front to place the bricks, as Figure 28 shows. To begin with, no more than three bricks at a time are used. As Brick Building progresses and the child's understanding increases, more bricks are gradually added until you are using as many as 10 to 12 bricks.

Brick building is first introduced as a Pairing activity, to help the child become familiar with and discriminate the different brick shapes:

- Put three bricks of different shapes on your own tray and three bricks identical to yours on the child's tray.

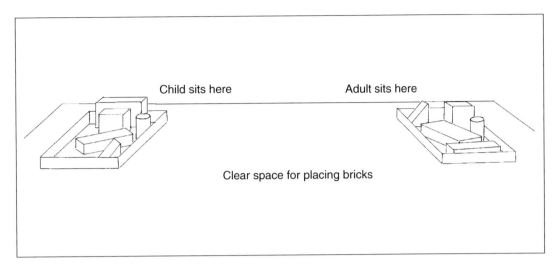

Child sits here   Adult sits here

Clear space for placing bricks

FIGURE 28 INTRODUCING BRICK BUILDING.

- Put one of your bricks in front of you on the table – this is the model brick.

- Point to it and help the child to pick up an identical brick from their tray, placing it on the table in front of them, and clearly separate from the model brick.

- Return the model brick to the tray, and then help the child to pick up their brick, returning it to their tray, simply saying 'Put the brick away'.

- Continue like this, using the same three bricks a number of times before changing them for three different ones. Continue to change them every so often, but keep to three bricks at this stage.

- Eventually, the child will start to anticipate, picking up their brick almost at the same time as you do, placing it on the table themselves.

- You can increase the number of bricks to four and then to six.

- When you feel the child is ready, extend the activity by leaving the bricks on the table this time, placing each new brick in front of the last one, making a row of bricks. The child does the same, making their own row of bricks, as shown in Figure 29.

- Once all the bricks on the tray have been used, say 'Put them away'. Both you and the child return the bricks to the respective trays.

- Give the child plenty of practice making these rows of bricks in preparation for true Brick Building.

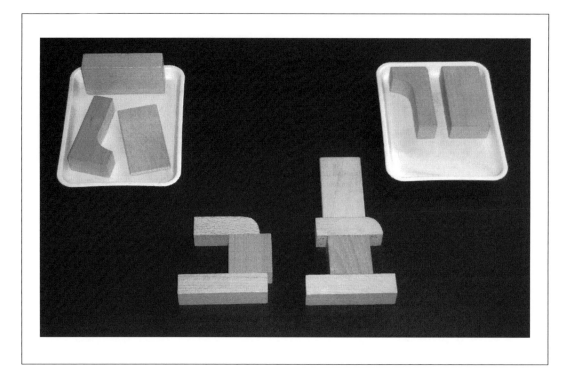

FIGURE 29 BRICK BUILDING – MAKING A ROW OF BRICKS.

12.5 BRICK BUILDING FROM A MODEL

Once the child can confidently identify the individual bricks, you can move on to true Brick Building. The object of the Brick Building activity is to encourage the child to make a praxic analysis and synthesis, in other words working out how the model is made by trying to build one. The result may not be an exact copy, but every attempt the child makes is a step on the way to understanding spatial relationships, making discoveries about relative position, direction, distance and orientation.

- Start the Brick Building with six bricks on your tray and six identical bricks on the child's tray.

- Make a simple two-brick model, for example one brick on top of the other, or one brick beside the other, etc.

- The child chooses the same two bricks and tries to place them in the same arrangement on the table in front of them, and clearly separate from your model. Some children will try to join their bricks onto your model; if this happens, help the child to move the bricks so that their structure is quite clearly separate from yours.

- Once their structure is made, you can say 'Put the bricks away', and both you and the child return the bricks one at a time to the trays. There is no need for more language. This is a continuous process of

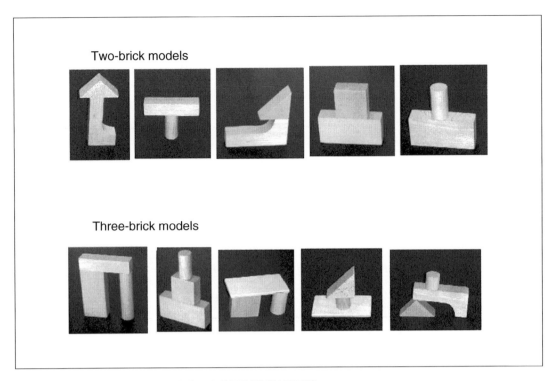

FIGURE 30 BRICK BUILDING – TWO-BRICK AND THREE-BRICK MODELS.

construction and removal that increases potential experience, and reduces any chance of the child becoming anxious.

- Make different combinations of two-brick models until you think the child is ready to try three-brick models – Figure 30 shows some examples. Then gradually increase the number of bricks used for each model, to help the child gain experience of as many arrangements as possible.

- You need to continually vary the models so that the child does not simply learn a particular structure by rote.

- If the child needs help making models with larger numbers of bricks, they can build their structure simultaneously with yours, so that each time you add a brick to your model the child adds a brick to their structure.

There may well be discrepancies in the early stages of this activity, for instance the child might make a mirror image of your model. There is no need to make changes to the child's structure; you can simply accept it. It is important to be flexible in finding ways to help the child so that they do not feel any sense of failure. For example, you can make a point of touching a particular brick on your model, to help the child find the next brick to add to their own structure. Or, you can deliberately pick up and replace a brick from your model once or twice, to alert the child to which brick to choose and where to put it. These are all ways of helping to maintain the momentum of the activity and to prevent confusion, if the child has inadvertently picked up a brick that is not the same as the

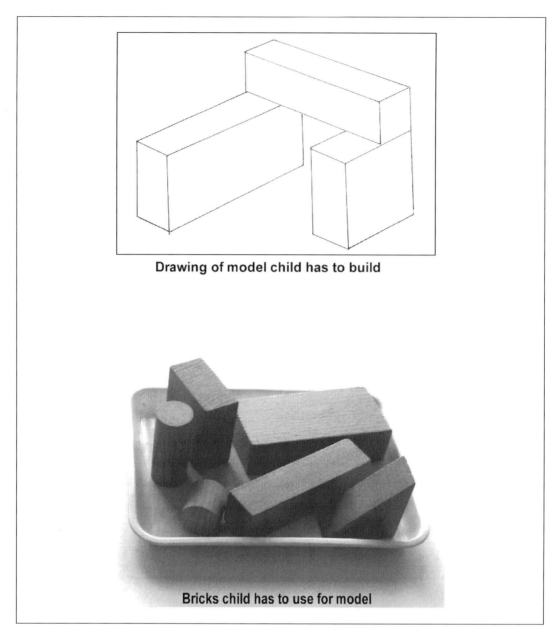

Drawing of model child has to build

Bricks child has to use for model

FIGURE 31 BRICK BUILDING – MAKING A BRICK MODEL FROM A DRAWING.

one on the model. Putting the bricks away as soon as a model is completed also maintains the momentum and avoids anxiety.

You can give the child time to use the bricks spontaneously at the end of the session. Or you can switch roles, getting the child to make a model for you to copy. This can make the activity very creative, flexible and pleasurable, with language and communication becoming a functional part of the Brick Building.

12.6 LINK WITH DRAWING

A drawing is a two-dimensional equivalent of a brick model, with lines and spaces representing three-dimensional structures. The drawings start with a single brick and work up to three- or four-brick models, like the example shown in Figure 31. You can put the drawing flat on the table, but at times it may help to hold it upright, making it easier for the child to relate it to the brick structure. To start with, you may need to help the child to find each of the bricks shown on the drawing before building the structure. The bricks in the drawings are shown in several different orientations, so the child has to recognize a brick as the same, although it may look different, for instance when seen from the side compared to the front. For the child who has already had a wide range of experience in Brick Building, this additional activity helps to increase spatial awareness.

12.7 EVERYDAY PLAY ACTIVITIES RELATED TO BRICK BUILDING

Brick Building in Functional Learning sessions can be extended into everyday play activities with construction toys familiar to most children. If possible, at home parents can provide a large bucket of bricks of different kinds for children to explore themselves, building and dismantling their own constructions. For those children whose coordination is well enough developed, there are toys like Lego, available in a large size which is a bit easier to handle, as well as a smaller size for those children who can manage finer movements. Children can put the Lego pieces together from an idea they have themselves, and later on from an illustrated model. Nurseries and schools also have similar types of play equipment for constructing things, which children with developmental delay can now begin to explore.

SECTION III

EXTENDING THE LEARNING ACTIVITIES

The bringing together of the earliest Learning Tools supports the development of later learning. The activities of Coding and Intersectional Sorting help children develop culturally appropriate behaviour and ways of thinking and organizing information. The extension of all the Learning Tools onto worksheets encourages independent learning. Children with developmental delay can begin to participate in daily classroom activities.

13

Coding

13.1 WHAT IS CODING?

Coding is a convention, or useful skill, used in a variety of ways in our society. 'The capacity to associate signs or actions in an arbitrary way so that one can be used to represent the other underlies the process of coding and the conventional use of symbols' (Waldon, 1980). There is not necessarily any logic in a code so, for example, in the case of traffic lights, it is agreed that red means stop and green go. The code on clothes labels is generally understood and relates to how to care for the clothes. The icons on computer screens are another kind of code. Among the most complex codes are letters and numbers. In the case of letters, certain drawn shapes stand for certain sounds and, when grouped together, these shapes make a word which, in its turn, can stand for an object, an action or an idea. Numbers and mathematical symbols – for instance, the signs for adding, subtracting, multiplying, dividing and equals – are the codes used to represent and record data. The complexity of the coding involved in writing, and the understanding of the code in reading and number, make it clear that Sequencing or thinking sequentially, Matching and Sorting are needed in order to understand and use Coding.

13.2 CODING IN READING, WRITING AND NUMBER

The teaching of reading, writing and maths are all vast topics in themselves, and it is not the purpose of this book to go into them in detail. But what is relevant here is the foundation of learning that children need, to be able to read and write and use numbers. There does seem to be general agreement that, in learning to read, children have to understand the alphabetic code and to learn the letter-sound correspondences (Thompson et al., 1993). In learning to write and spell, they need to make sense of the codes and conventions of letters and sounds and the idiosyncrasies of spelling (Czerniewska, 1992). Children also need to be able to use the words for numbers and mathematical symbols, and to write them, that is, they need to know the code. Of course, they must also have a broad base of experience of the world around them to facilitate understanding of what they read and write, and experience of everyday objects and concrete materials to enable them to make the link between the abstract numerical code and the real world. But the focus here is the coding element of these areas of learning. Activities to help children with developmental delay use Coding will support future learning to read, write and use number.

13.3 CODING AND CHILDREN WITH DEVELOPMENTAL DELAY

Coding seems to start very early in the life of the normally developing child, with simple associations between things that happen by chance. The way the baby learns to sort out the mother's face, linking her presence with a special sound, or perhaps food and comfort, could be seen as one of the first associations. In early coding, the child begins to understand that one thing consistently stands for another. Already, by age four, children can understand symbols representing roads, rivers and parks on a map (Robson, 2006). Eventually, they can use the symbolic mode of representation and develop an understanding of symbols, signs and numbers. Symbols are used in a flexible way: things do not remain fixed.

Children with developmental delay, however, prefer to keep things the same – their thinking is not flexible. But a Functional Learning programme helps to reduce the fear of change and the secondary defensive behaviours are dropped. Pairing, Matching, Sorting and Sequencing are developed to a mature level. Along with the development of the Learning Tools the delayed child acquires flexible thinking. So, for example, when the ability to code is used in the process of reading, it allows for a greater flexibility in the use of symbols, showing a progression from dependence on the concrete, physical properties of things to an ability to use abstract signs.

It is helpful for children with developmental delay to acquire at least a basic level of symbolic language and symbolic signs, in order to be able to respond with culturally appropriate behaviour. Prior to the introduction of Coding, mature Matching familiarizes the child with the idea of a symbol standing for something, such as the word 'dog' representing or standing for a picture of a dog, the picture and word in turn standing for a real dog.

13.4 MATERIALS FOR CODING

Because Coding involves something that stands for something else, a key card, providing the key to the code, has to be supplied, similar to the way a legend for a map is needed to be able to understand the map. The key card has two rows of spaces drawn on it, resembling the Pairing/Matching boards. The top row of spaces shows, for example, the shapes or colours (symbols) of the code and the bottom row indicates what the colours or shapes stand for – for example, blue represents a house, red represents a car, green a tree, etc. Sets of cards are created made of the same type of thick card and 5 cm square, the same size as all the other cards used in Functional Learning activities. In each set, there are cards with the symbols on – in the example, circles coloured blue, red, green, etc. – and cards showing what the various symbols stand for – house, car, tree, etc. The boards used for Pairing/Matching are also used for Coding activities. Figure 32 shows one way of setting out the Coding materials.

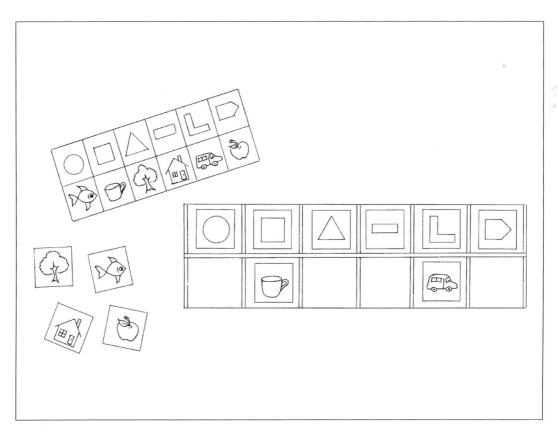

FIGURE 32 CODING – KEY CARD, CARDS AND BOARD.

FIGURE 33 SIMPLE CODING.

13.5 SIMPLE CODING

You need to give the child a key card, showing the key to the code, and a Pairing/Matching board. Put the cards showing the code symbols along the top row of spaces on the board. Then put in place on the bottom row of spaces on the board some of the cards illustrating the objects the symbols stand for. This is equivalent to seeding in the Sorting activity, explained in 10.4. Put the other cards, needed to fill the spaces on the bottom row, nearby on the table. Help the child to point to an empty space on the board with one hand, using the other hand to point first to the symbol above this space, and then to the symbol and the object it stands for on the key card. Having found the card with the appropriate object, the child puts it under the symbol on the board, as Figure 33 shows. While the pointing finger can keep the child focused on the symbol and the object related to that symbol, the child also needs to be able to keep two things in mind.

For this initial Coding, the symbols need to be kept simple and clear; drawn outlines of shapes or distinctive colours are good choices, as the example on the CD shows. The objects the symbols stand for also need to be clearly different from each other, for example a circle could stand for a cup, a square for a chair, a triangle for a car, etc. To have makes of cars or varieties of chairs at this stage would be too complex.

13.6 INTERMEDIATE CODING

Once the basic idea of something standing for something else is understood, seeding will not be necessary. You can use cards to stand for actual objects, so two-dimensional symbols represent three-dimensional objects. At this stage, you could introduce symbols standing for actions, for example pictures of walking, running, jumping, swimming and skipping. The symbols used for these actions could be colours or shapes which have been used in other contexts, but by now the child understands that the use of symbols is flexible.

13.7 MATURE CODING

With mature Coding, codes can be used to relate to various objects in a particular set, so a set of woodwork tools could be coded for hammer, chisel, saw, etc. You can introduce Coding worksheets (see Chapter 15). Some children will be able to invent their own codes. When they can undertake this kind of independent work and communicate more freely, children can use Coding to record information about everyday activities or instructions relating to other Functional Learning tasks.

As Coding is a useful tool in everyday life, it is important for the child to have the opportunity to see it in use. Road signs, map symbols, certain food containers like milk cartons, and different values of postage stamps all use Coding. Children with developmental delay who are able to use and understand these codes can now relate them to the world around them.

14

Intersectional Sorting

14.1 WHAT IS INTERSECTIONAL SORTING?

In Intersectional Sorting, a grid is used to bring together two or more pieces of information contained in objects, pictures or cards. The result or 'answer' produced by bringing together the information is shown where the relevant rows and columns of squares on the grid meet, or intersect. Intersectional Sorting is not an end in itself but a way of helping the child to use information for problem solving. Using a grid where information can be put together, taken apart and otherwise transformed involves seeing relationships and associations between various pieces of information – an ability needed for causal thinking. The grid also enables the child to see that the whole is the sum total of the parts.

Normally developing children around five to six years of age are usually able to work out what to do when presented with the Intersectional Sorting boards and cards. Before starting Intersectional Sorting, a child must be able to 'chain' in every direction (for an explanation of 'chaining', see 11.5) and to use both hands independently. They must have the ability to place accurately, to pair, to match and to sort at a conceptual level. The child also needs to be able to make a decision and change it as more information becomes available, to scan and to ignore 'noise' in the form of potentially distracting information.

14.2 MATERIALS FOR INTERSECTIONAL SORTING

▨ INTERSECTIONAL SORTING BOARDS

Intersectional Sorting is carried out on a grid marked out on a board made of a sturdy material such as hardboard. Each space on the grid is approximately 6 cm square. On the early, simple-stage board, the grid is made of thin strips of wood marking out well-defined spaces for the objects or cards. A border or frame around the grid forms a clear boundary between the axis objects or cards and the spaces of the grid itself.

For a middle, or intermediate, stage board, you can draw the grid on the board, still with a frame around it, which you can also draw in. When the child is used to the drawn grid, you can move on to a final, mature stage board where the grid and spaces for axis cards are drawn right up to the edge of the board. The number of spaces on the grid varies with the progression of activities. Figure 34 illustrates the different boards.

▨ OBJECTS FOR INTERSECTIONAL SORTING

Objects can be used to introduce Intersectional Sorting, particularly for those children who have had little experience of this kind of problem solving. When choosing objects, it is worth keeping in mind that they need to fit the spaces on the grid and remain stable, so that they will not roll or fall over, and they should have qualities that can be used on the grid, such as colour, shape, size, number, etc. Examples of suitable objects are small bricks, buttons, coloured plastic cotton reels and flat plastic shapes, but there are all sorts of other possibilities, and the CD illustrates just a few.

▨ CARDS FOR INTERSECTIONAL SORTING

Once the child is familiar with using the board and has understood how to combine information from the axis objects, in order to find which object goes in each square of the grid, the next stage is to begin using cards. You can make sets of cards cut from thick craft card; all cards are the same size – 5 cm square – so that they are interchangeable. The CD illustrates some possible sets.

14.3 SIMPLE INTERSECTIONAL SORTING

▨ CHAINING

Use objects to start with, before going on to sets of cards. First, help the child to chain objects on the board, placing them in single (horizontal) rows, working from right to left and sometimes left to right, or (vertical) columns, working from top to bottom and sometimes bottom to top. The chaining is done before

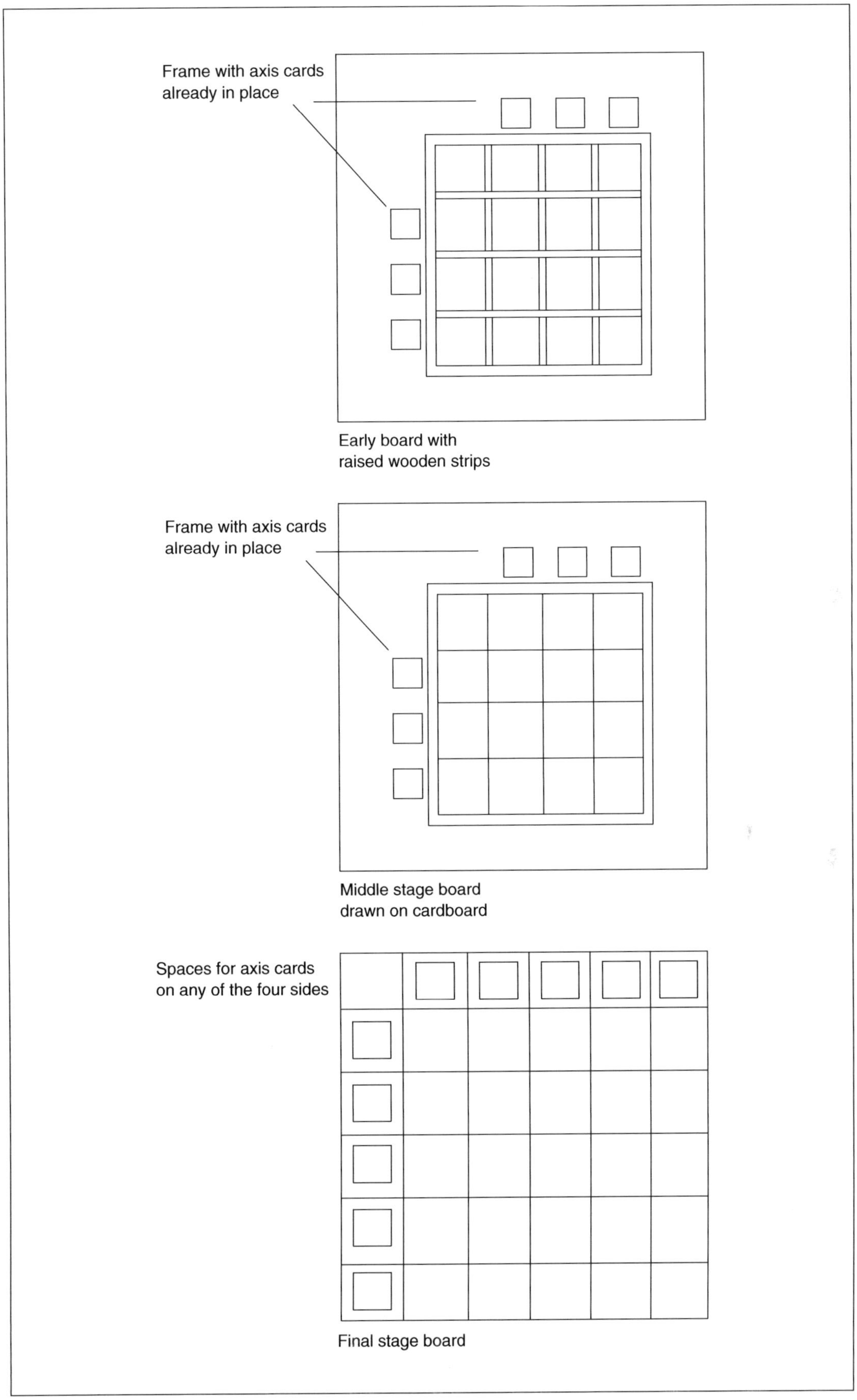

Frame with axis cards
already in place

Early board with
raised wooden strips

Frame with axis cards
already in place

Middle stage board
drawn on cardboard

Spaces for axis cards
on any of the four sides

Final stage board

FIGURE 34 INTERSECTIONAL SORTING – SIMPLE, INTERMEDIATE AND MATURE STAGE BOARDS.

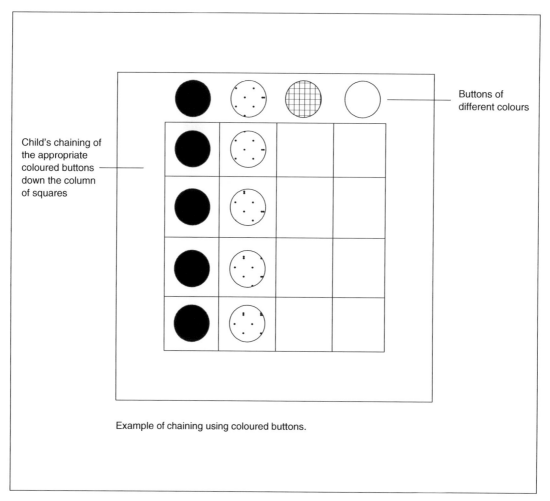

Child's chaining of the appropriate coloured buttons down the column of squares

Buttons of different colours

Example of chaining using coloured buttons.

FIGURE 35 SIMPLE INTERSECTIONAL SORTING – CHAINING.

introducing the idea of combining the information from a row and a column to make an intersection.

Set out a series of objects, perhaps different coloured buttons, along one edge of the board. The child makes a chain up or down the columns or across the row of squares with the relevant coloured button. Both the left-hand and right-hand edges of the board, as well as the bottom edge, are used in turn as the axis, so that the chaining is done in all directions. Many different objects can be used like this until the child can chain confidently. Figure 35 shows an example of chaining.

INTERSECTIONAL SORTING WITH OBJECTS

In the initial stages, Intersectional Sorting is limited to the bringing together of two elements of information to one square on the grid. With objects this means, for example, if there are colours down one axis and shapes along the other axis, the answer on the grid is a coloured shape. To help the child understand this combining of information, you will need to give them plenty of practice using objects as a pre-card technique. One advantage of using objects is that the actual relationship between two elements can be seen, for example a peg on top of a cotton reel or a button beside a brick.

It will help the child to understand the combining of two pieces of information if they point to an object on one axis with one hand and an object on the other axis with the other hand. One pointing finger then moves along a row and the other along a column, until they meet on the square where the row and column intersects. The child leaves one finger on that square while finding the object to go on it, from a pile of objects set out to one side of the board.

14.4 INTERMEDIATE INTERSECTIONAL SORTING

Once the child is confident using objects, you can introduce sets of cards, at first relatively simple, for example bringing together two clearly defined shapes so that both shapes appear in the answer on the intersection square. In addition to

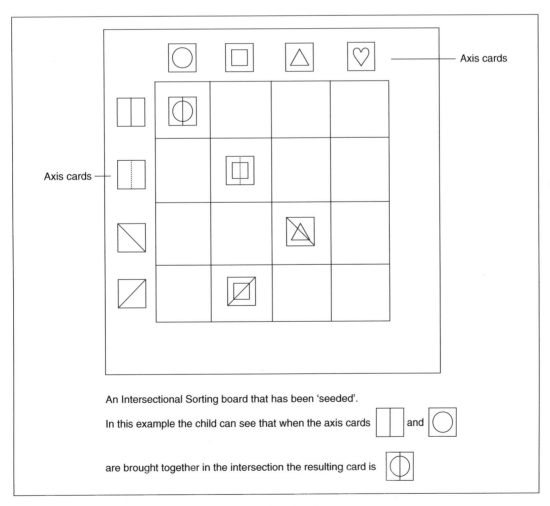

FIGURE 36 INTERMEDIATE INTERSECTIONAL SORTING – SEEDED BOARD.

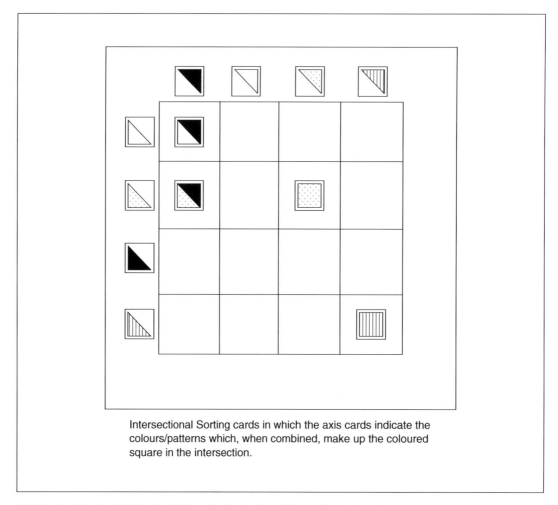

Intersectional Sorting cards in which the axis cards indicate the colours/patterns which, when combined, make up the coloured square in the intersection.

FIGURE 37 INTERMEDIATE INTERSECTIONAL SORTING – COMBINING COLOUR AND PATTERN.

using the pointing finger, it may help the child if the board is 'seeded', so that some cards are already placed in the intersection squares, as shown in Figure 36. The other cards needed to fill the spaces on the grid are placed in a pile to one side, ready for the child to pick up and look at one card at a time, then find its place on the grid.

Eventually, the child will be ready to use more complex cards, where combining information from the axis cards produces a result that no longer closely resembles the individual elements, or shapes, as shown in Figure 37.

14.5 MATURE INTERSECTIONAL SORTING

INTEGRATED SHAPES

As the child progresses to mature Intersectional Sorting, the elements, or shapes, are brought closer together in the answer, so that the child has to understand increasingly complex and integrated shapes (see Figure 38). It is important to consider the type of board used as well as the level of complexity of the

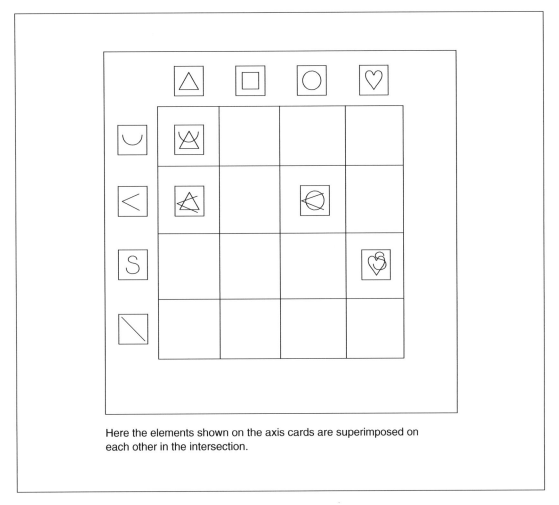

Here the elements shown on the axis cards are superimposed on each other in the intersection.

FIGURE 38 MATURE INTERSECTIONAL SORTING – SUPERIMPOSED SHAPES.

information on the cards. If the child can use an intermediate stage board, you can make the card material less complex initially. You will need to monitor the child's response as you move between the different boards and adjust the complexity of the card material, until the child can use a final stage board with any degree of complexity of information.

ORIENTATION

The orientation of the elements on the axis cards is a dimension that can either be used or ignored when completing the intersection, as illustrated in Figures 39 and 40.

SOURCE AND AMOUNT OF INFORMATION

Using a final stage board, you can distribute the axis cards, which hold information, between the four sides of the board. This gives the child experience of dealing with information coming from various sources (see Figure 41). You could also have six axis cards on each side of the board, which means the child has to manage increasing amounts of information.

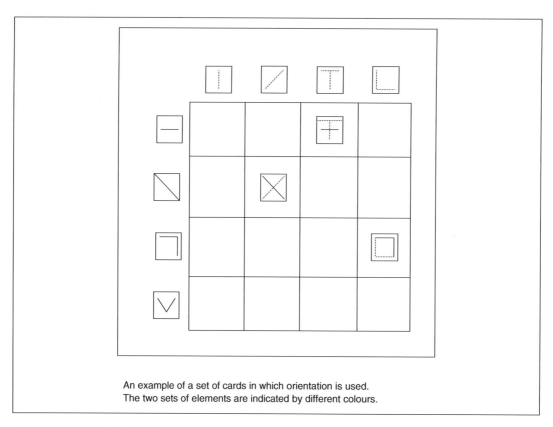

An example of a set of cards in which orientation is used.
The two sets of elements are indicated by different colours.

FIGURE 39 MATURE INTERSECTIONAL SORTING – USING ORIENTATION.

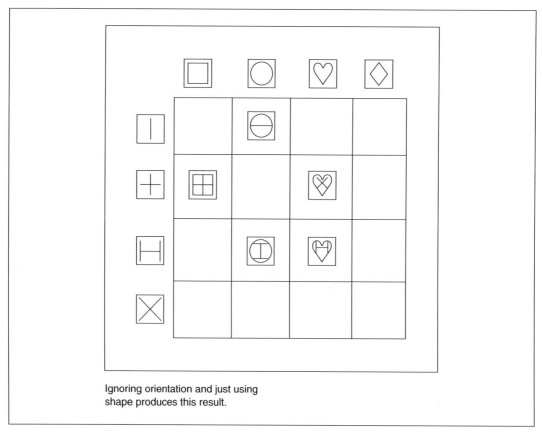

Ignoring orientation and just using
shape produces this result.

FIGURE 40 MATURE INTERSECTIONAL SORTING – IGNORING ORIENTATION.

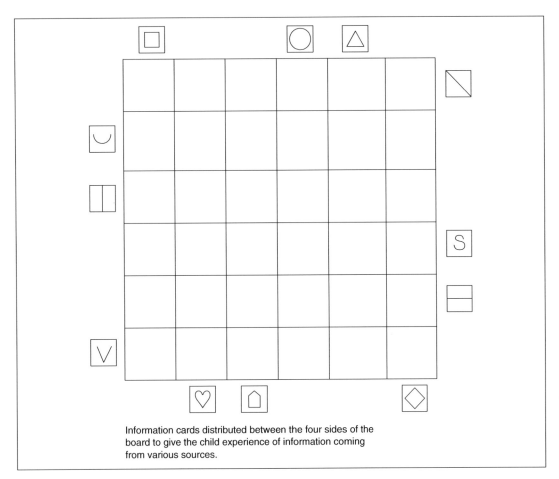

Information cards distributed between the four sides of the board to give the child experience of information coming from various sources.

FIGURE 41 MATURE INTERSECTIONAL SORTING – INFORMATION FROM MULTIPLE SOURCES.

SEEDING

The intersectional information can simply come from extensive seeding of the grid, as shown in Figure 42.

EXTRA CARDS

Another variation you can introduce is to have more cards available than spaces on the grid. As the child works their way through the cards, finding the card for each square, the spare cards are gradually eliminated.

WRITTEN INFORMATION

You can give the child written information on the cards rather than just symbols. There are several ways of doing this. The information on the axis cards can be given in words, for example blue, yellow, green, etc. on one axis and dog, car, etc. on the other, and the answer on the grid is an object – a yellow dog, a green dog, a blue car, and so on. The information can also be given using objects and the answer is a written card – 'green car' or 'blue square'. The objects can be removed altogether and just written cards used.

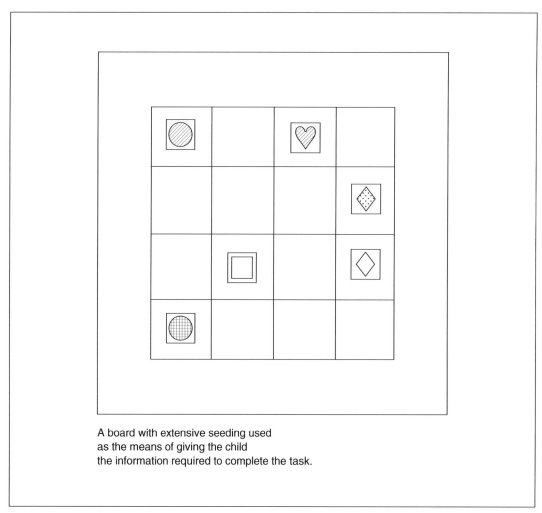

A board with extensive seeding used
as the means of giving the child
the information required to complete the task.

FIGURE 42 MATURE INTERSECTIONAL SORTING – INFORMATION FROM SEEDED CARDS.

■ 'TAKING AWAY' GAMES

During the later stages of Intersectional Sorting, two children can join in 'taking away' games. While one child closes their eyes, the other child takes away and hides one or two cards from the grid. The first child now has to say, or draw, which cards have been removed. By this time, the child is bringing together all elements in the form of two written pieces of information in order to explore number, size, position, colour, etc.

■ 'MISSING ELEMENTS'

Working out answers to problems not only consists of taking note of the information we already have, but also involves finding what other information we need. 'Missing elements' in Intersectional Sorting focuses on this idea of missing information. When introducing 'missing elements', you can limit the number of elements to just four, on a board that is three squares by three squares. As the child is competent enough by this stage to be able to use a board where the grid squares are only drawn in, this new grid can be drawn on very firm card. More elements of

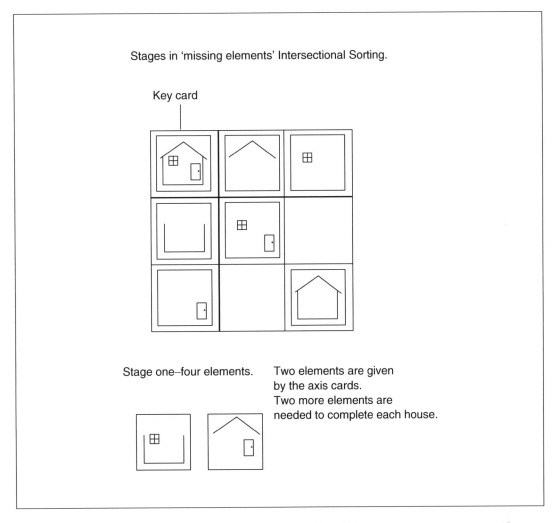

Stages in 'missing elements' Intersectional Sorting.

Key card

Stage one–four elements.

Two elements are given
by the axis cards.
Two more elements are
needed to complete each house.

FIGURE 43 MATURE INTERSECTIONAL SORTING – MISSING ELEMENTS STAGE 1.

information can be added later, and then you will need to draw a new board increasing the number of squares.

You need to provide a key card that shows the complete solution. The axis cards show one or two of the elements involved, and the card that goes in the intersection shows the element that is missing when both axis cards are brought together. When the two axis cards provide all the elements needed, the card that goes in the intersection is a blank. Later, the elements are so arranged on the axis cards that the child may have two roofs and one set of walls, but still needs a door and a window to make one complete house. It is important to include this step to help the child understand that an excess of one element – in this case, two roofs – does not solve the problem. Figures 43, 44 and 45 show the different stages of 'missing elements'.

ANSWERING QUESTIONS

Finally, when this degree of sophistication in Intersectional Sorting is reached, you can give the child a grid with information on all four sides. The information could be pets, ages, colour of eyes, colour of hair, or objects

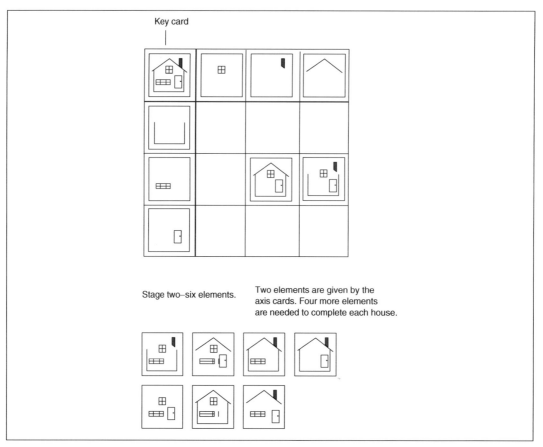

FIGURE 44 MATURE INTERSECTIONAL SORTING – MISSING ELEMENTS STAGE 2.

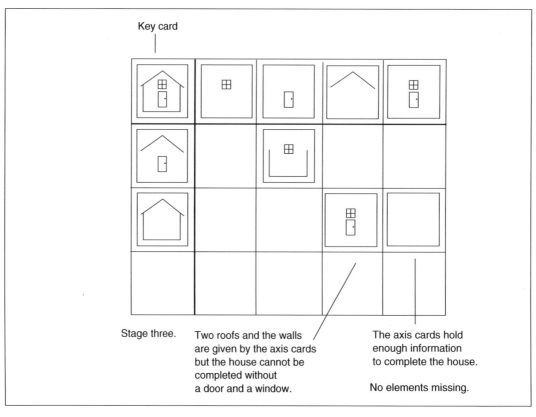

FIGURE 45 MATURE INTERSECTIONAL SORTING – MISSING ELEMENTS STAGE 3.

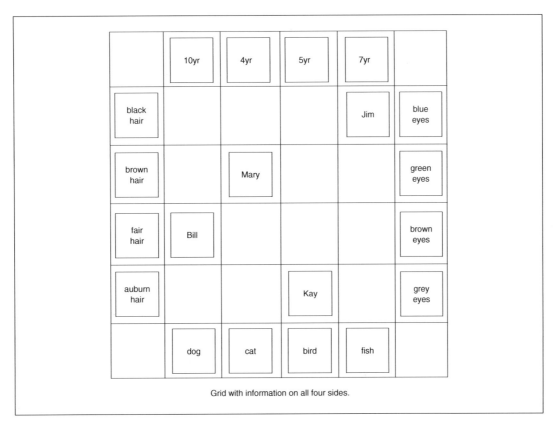

	10yr	4yr	5yr	7yr	
black hair				Jim	blue eyes
brown hair		Mary			green eyes
fair hair	Bill				brown eyes
auburn hair			Kay		grey eyes
	dog	cat	bird	fish	

Grid with information on all four sides.

FIGURE 46 MATURE INTERSECTIONAL SORTING – USING A GRID TO ANSWER QUESTIONS.

owned, as shown in Figure 46. With the names on the grid, you can ask the child questions such as 'How old is Mary?' In fact, the child can be asked questions involving all or any of the various elements around the board. With several names on the grid, some elements may be shared with two or more people, which can give rise to other types of questions. Clearly, at this stage, language has become an integral part of the activity.

14.6 EXTENSION OF INTERSECTIONAL SORTING

WORKSHEETS

You can use worksheets to extend the activity at each stage of Intersectional Sorting. So, for simple Intersectional Sorting, the worksheet may have colour on one axis and shape along the other, and the child has to draw a coloured shape in the appropriate square on the grid. The grids on the worksheets can be seeded by having some of the squares already completed. You may need to find a way of making sure that the child does not simply fill in whole rows of one element at a time. One way of randomizing the filling in of grids on worksheets, and encouraging continued decision making, is to number each square. The child must then follow that order, crossing off the number each time on a checklist, as shown in Figure 47.

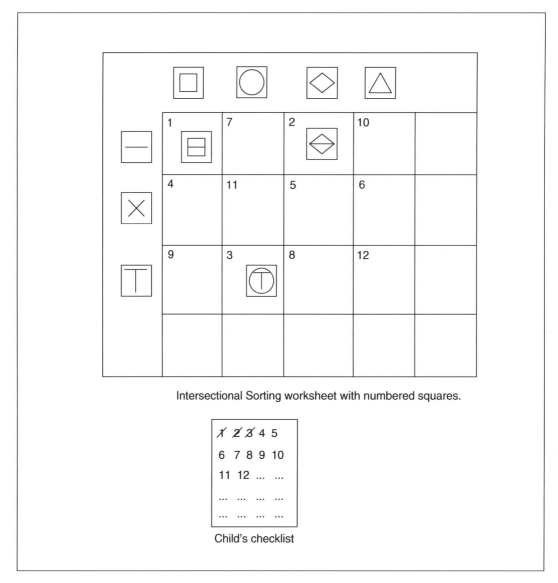

Intersectional Sorting worksheet with numbered squares.

Child's checklist

FIGURE 47 INTERSECTIONAL SORTING WORKSHEET.

USING A GRID

The grid itself can be used to organize an accumulation of information which needs to be tabulated to facilitate the solving of a problem. For example, you could give the child a mass of information about a set of people, to be tabulated by placing the various names down one side of the grid and the information across the top. A tick or a cross in the appropriate square indicates whether the information above the square applies to a particular person or not (see Figure 48). Questions, such as 'Who likes oranges but not apples?' or 'How many children dislike pears?', can then be answered.

USING INTERSECTIONAL POINTS

Use of the intersectional grid is endless. Not only can the intersection squares be used but also the intersectional points where lines cross.

Fruit eaten

	oranges	apples	pears	grapes
Peter	✓	✗	✓	✗
Jane	✓	✓	✗	✗
Bill	✗	✓	✗	✓

Example of how a grid can be used to convey information.

Key: ✓ = likes
x = dislikes

FIGURE 48 INFORMATION ON A GRID.

Intersectional points can be used to draw large shapes or show the rotation of a line, as illustrated in Figures 49 and 50. Graphs can also be drawn, or the reading of a map grid can be developed. The possibilities are indeed endless.

▓ INFORMATION TO SOLVE PROBLEMS

The elements of information that are brought together in the Intersectional Sorting activities are in close proximity to one another. But this is not necessarily the case for information needed to solve problems in everyday life, which may require looking in many different places. To help children gain this experience, they can be moved on, through the worksheets and simple information books, to finding and bringing together information from much wider sources. You can ask the child to look at a certain page in a book, then at two pages and, eventually, two or even more books, and perhaps books that are kept in different places, bringing together the information gathered.

14.7 LEARNING TO THINK

Although using a grid may be a common activity, the unique contribution of Intersectional Sorting is the way it has been developed to provide a progression

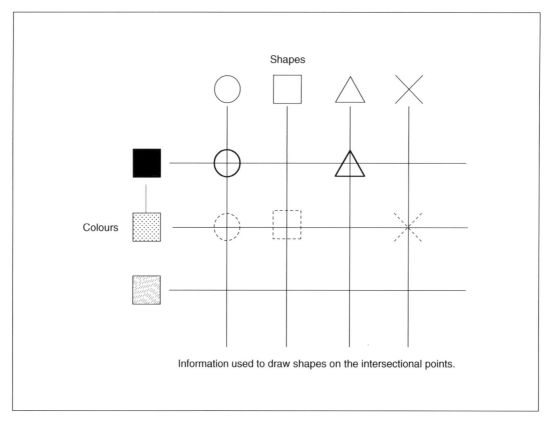

Information used to draw shapes on the intersectional points.

FIGURE 49 USING INTERSECTIONAL POINTS TO DRAW SHAPES.

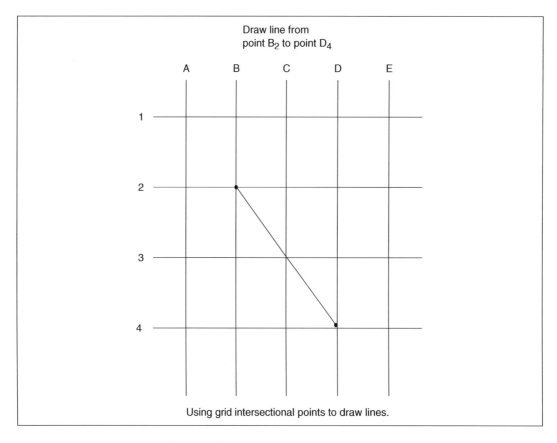

Using grid intersectional points to draw lines.

FIGURE 50 USING INTERSECTIONAL POINTS TO DRAW A LINE.

of activities, from the simplest chaining of objects all the way to using the written information on a grid to answer questions. Children learn to abstract information and combine ideas. It helps with the ability to understand causal relationships – if I do this, then that will happen. It gives children a simple method of organizing what may on the face of it seem like very complex information within a space that they can comprehend. Intersectional Sorting has its own intrinsic interest and satisfaction for children but, much more than that, it helps them develop a way of thinking and dealing with information that will aid problem solving in many different life situations.

15

Worksheets

CONTENTS

- An educational tool

- Introducing worksheets

- Organizing the information

- Working independently

- Worksheets to extend the Learning Tools

15.1 AN EDUCATIONAL TOOL

Worksheets are commonly used in the classroom as an educational tool. A wide range of workbooks is commercially available with similar activities to those done with worksheets, for parents to help support their child's learning at home. All these activities help children practise and consolidate their Learning Tools, develop confidence and encourage independent learning. A milestone has been reached when worksheets can be introduced to children with developmental delay, as they can begin to participate in the activities of mainstream education.

15.2 INTRODUCING WORKSHEETS

When introducing worksheets, it is important to take into account that many children with developmental delay are fearful of putting marks on paper, because of their anxiety when faced with the unfamiliar and their experiences of failure in the past. For some children, the marks represent something that will always be there and they find it quite threatening. It can be helpful for children to make marks in sand first. They can use a small tray of sand and, each time they make marks, they can shake the tray so that the marks disappear. The work done in Banging and Scraping will help children to make large, free marks on paper. Once children do progress to working with paper and pencil on worksheets, they will need to be able to make more precise marks, placed with accuracy. Using a pencil and a rubber will help reduce the anxiety, because they will have a way of removing what they have done.

15.3 ORGANIZING THE INFORMATION

Throughout the Functional Learning process, measures are taken to cut down 'noise' or distraction, and the working surface is kept clear, except for the activity the child is doing. Worksheets also need to be set out so that they are clear and uncluttered. Too much on the sheet and the child will be overwhelmed. We all get the same feeling when faced with a form with too much information, and to help reduce the confusion, we may use strategies like following the text with our finger. The child too can be encouraged to use this pointing strategy.

15.4 WORKING INDEPENDENTLY

During the Functional Learning activities, to help establish the Learning Tools, there has necessarily been a lot of support. Worksheets can give children the opportunity to work on their own, although someone still needs to be at hand in case the child needs help. The worksheets can be left waiting on a child's table, so that they feel their presence has been anticipated and each individual has been carefully provided for. Examples of worksheets described are found on the CD, together with further information about using them.

15.5 WORKSHEETS TO EXTEND THE LEARNING TOOLS

PAIRING AND MATCHING

The simplest form of worksheet is based on Pairing and Matching. To start with, use three or four pairs only. The two items that make up a pair, cups for example, are shown on either side of the sheet. For children who are only just beginning to use worksheets, the items are directly opposite each other, which is more like Pairing, but later on they can be out of sequence so that it becomes more like Matching. To help the child in the early stages, you can complete one set of items on the worksheet as an example of what to do. The child indicates the other pairs by joining them with a line. As the child becomes more competent, you can increase the number of items on the worksheet and introduce more complexity, until eventually words are matched with pictures or numbers with a collection of drawn objects.

PENCIL MANIPULATION

The child needs to be able to manipulate a pencil in increasingly complex ways. You can design worksheets with various 'writing patterns' and, for example, get the child to draw through a maze. These activities can be great fun and make learning a pleasure.

SORTING

For worksheets based on Sorting, drawn objects or shapes are spread all over the sheet of paper, the number of sets of course being limited to some extent by the size of the paper. At the top or bottom of the page, or down the side, are a number of squares or circles, equivalent to the containers used in sorting objects and cards. They need to be 'seeded' with examples of the items to be sorted. By drawing a line from each item to the relevant 'container', the child indicates which set it belongs to.

SEQUENCING

The simplest Sequencing worksheet is a two-element, repeating sequence where the child has to colour in a row of shapes, for instance blue, then red repeated. The first three or four shapes are already coloured in, equivalent to the 'trail' of objects set out in a Sequencing session. This means the worksheet has all the information on it that the child needs.

From this simple start, the sequences can increase in complexity – you can increase the number of elements, use more than one sequence on the sheet, and have sequences that explore increasing and decreasing size or number. A sequence can follow a simple action, such as an object being pushed into a container. Where the child has to fill in gaps in any of the sequences, each element of the sequence needs to be clearly defined, for example by drawn squares. The child then knows that the empty square is a gap that they have to fill in the sequence.

BRICK BUILDING

On Brick Building worksheets, the child has to copy a drawn shape. It is helpful if each line that makes up the completed shape is in a different colour. The different coloured lines are equivalent to indicating the different bricks needed in the Brick Building session, either by a built model or a drawn plan. Start with simple shapes because the child now has to create shapes themselves.

CODING

You need to provide a key on the worksheet, the same as you would for the Coding activity. On the sheet, draw a grid resembling the Pairing boards, with a number of squares already filled in. The child then completes the empty squares with the help of the key.

INTERSECTIONAL SORTING

The information on the worksheet is set out in the same way as it appears on the Intersectional Sorting board. Activities are also the same as when using board and cards, but the child creates the 'answer' by drawing, which makes the activity more complex. You can determine the order in which the child completes squares by numbering each square on the grid, and then giving the child a list of numbers indicating the sequence for completing the squares.

AND BEYOND

Once the basic Learning Tools have been established in the worksheet format, and the child has acquired more reading and writing skills, the scope of the worksheets can be extended. The child can fill in missing words in a simple text, which requires both sequencing the sense or events of the sentence, and sorting out the relevant word from the possible candidates for the space. Sorting by the criteria of where objects are found would be required to answer the question, 'I collected seashells on my holiday. Did I have a holiday by the sea or in the country?'. In the end, the challenge will be to think of ideas to create a good supply of worksheets.

Turning the worksheets into a 'book' needs to be given careful thought. We all tend to assume that things get more difficult as we progress through a book. A sheet at the end that is too difficult might even prevent the child starting the book at all, so the last worksheets in the book need to be well within the child's competence.

SECTION IV

COMMUNICATION, EMOTIONAL GROWTH AND THE FAMILY

These three chapters are about families living and working with their developmentally delayed children – the integration of learning and language, the emotional problems and the difficult behaviour. It describes the different kind of parenting needed and supports the idea of working in collaboration with parents. Chapter 18 focuses on feeding, with an account illustrating a successful therapeutic intervention.

16

Language and Communication

CONTENTS

♦ Early communication

♦ Communication and the child with developmental delay

♦ Some early intervention strategies

♦ The staircase routine

♦ Body language and protective behaviour

♦ Therapeutic language

♦ Integration of language and learning: case study

16.1 EARLY COMMUNICATION

The earliest pre-verbal communication between parents and their baby is a mutual gazing accompanied by simultaneous vocalizing. The pointing gesture is another early communication, with parent and infant looking in the direction of what they are pointing to, then looking at each other. In the first couple of months, babies make gurgling and cooing noises until, at about six months, babbling begins when they have enough muscle control to combine a consonant with a vowel sound. Pleasurable babbling games develop between parents and their child. Early words, which appear by about a year, grow out of the babble sounds. By the end of the second year, the infant has many words and is beginning to put words together (Bee and Boyd, 2004; Bloom, 1993; Stern, 1985).

16.2 COMMUNICATION AND THE CHILD WITH DEVELOPMENTAL DELAY

Some parents who have a child with developmental delay do experience an early intimate responsiveness between themselves and their child during the first few months, but others may not. All parents anticipate that there will be a change from the pre-verbal, body language communication to words and verbal expression. Parents who find that this has not happened by the time their child is a year old also become aware of limitations in their child's range of emotional expressiveness, and an increase in bouts of intense, prolonged crying.

Very often, when parents seek help for their child, their focus is on the child's inability to talk. Sometimes their desperate need for their child to talk understandably makes it more difficult for them to accept that language, understanding and cognitive growth are interconnected, and that language development can only be facilitated by working with all areas of development. As Bloom (1993) says, 'even though we may study them separately, language, cognition and emotion are fundamentally and systematically related'. Functional Learning integrates all aspects of development by helping the child to establish a firm foundation of learning and appropriate emotional responsiveness, from which comes increased understanding leading to the development of language. The last part of the video on the CD shows children who have participated in Functional Learning programmes now talking and responding appropriately.

16.3 SOME EARLY INTERVENTION STRATEGIES

For those children who have had little or no experience of baby babble, parents can begin to imitate early babble play – blowing bubbles, touching lips and tongue, finding opportunities for imitating mouth shapes using a mirror when appropriate, and increasing vocal play. Vowels and consonants, and eventually simple words, begin to emerge out of this repetitive babble play. Mealtimes can also be used to establish pleasurable contact when simple words and sounds can be introduced, such as 'Mmm, nice' or 'More'.

The repetition of 'm-m-m' and 'b-b-b', and then stretch of the lips to form a vowel 'i' and a wider open mouth to make 'o', can be extended to make word-like sounds, such as 'milk' and 'ball'. This will become meaningful if the child experiences the sounds repeatedly, in connection with drinking milk and with balls that can be placed one by one in a container, while helping the child to attempt the word-like sound each time. However fragile the sound is to begin with, this kind of game can be extremely pleasurable for both child and parent/carer. This essential practice and repetition of words in a meaningful context needs to continue on a daily basis with the family at home and, if possible, at nursery or school. It can also become an integral part of the Functional Learning sessions, although not during the learning activities themselves.

In the initial Functional Learning sessions, language is kept to a minimum during the learning activities, similar to the quiet, self-motivated activity of the child under two. It also enables the child to conserve cognitive resources for developing the early Learning Tools. Very often, language develops functionally from the Functional Learning activities, just as it does from the normal child's early exploration and play. On the CD video, Helen, at five, was sorting picture cards she had seen several times before. On recognizing the card with red stripes, she suddenly said 'stwipes'. This was not necessarily a social communication, as she did not look up at the adults in the room, but she was saying out loud, and with great pleasure, a word that had meaning for her.

16.4 THE STAIRCASE ROUTINE

Once they have the movement capability, young children are usually very keen to climb a staircase. The staircase routine takes advantage of this enthusiasm. It is an activity that can be both pleasurable and successful in helping children to start using single words associated with body movement, and to increase their body awareness in a functional way. It can be done with children who can walk up and down stairs holding on to a rail, or holding an adult's hand.

- To start with, you may need to have two people helping the child, one in front facing the child, the other beside or behind the child, to help the child move and make sure they are safe on the stairs.

- Start with the child at the bottom of the staircase. The person in front stands one or two steps further up the staircase in relation to the child, gesturing and saying 'up', and moving up one step each time the child takes a step. The other person helps the child to look at the adult in front and to move up one step, also moving up one step themselves each time, so that they are always beside or immediately behind the child.

- For children with very limited understanding, it may be necessary at first to help them move one or both feet to the next step.

- Some children want to rush up or down the stairs, without looking or listening. They need to be helped to change their focus to the word and the gesture, so that they can begin to develop their understanding in association with body movement.

- Particularly with a small child, when you are in front of the child, you may need to bend down so that you are more on a level with the child, or you can even sit on the step so that the child can see your face and your hand gesturing 'up'.

- Both gesture and word are repeated for each step, with the child moving only one step at a time.

- Continue the routine with 'down', pointing down and repeating the word for every step down.

- It may be some time before the child begins to use the gesture and eventually the words for 'up' and 'down'.

- With some children, you may need to help them move their lips to make a sound for 'up' or 'down' while they watch the person in front making the gesture.

- Once the child has mastered both the gesture and the word, the roles are reversed and the child experiences *you* responding to *their* word and gesture, realizing that their words can make things happen. If you have two people doing this, one person stands at the bottom of the stairs, while the other person stands with the child at the top of the stairs, helping the child to gesture and say 'up' and to wait each time for the person at the bottom to take a step up. The positions are reversed for coming down.

- This activity can be done at home, becoming a pleasurable game with other children in the family. And it can be done in nursery or school as a shared activity with other children.

16.5 BODY LANGUAGE AND PROTECTIVE BEHAVIOUR

Children who have not developed verbal communication often resort to using body language. Their fear, anxiety and frustration are all reflected in their behaviour. They may refuse to listen to what the adult is saying. They often withdraw from any social contact, sometimes by looking out of the window, or turning their body so their face cannot be seen, only showing their backs. They may become angry, or start screaming or crying, and sometimes use their body to attack others, biting, kicking, hitting or running away. These protective behaviours are part of the strategies they develop to defend themselves against their lack of understanding. They are sometimes more difficult to change than the primary causes of language delay, and there are children who may continue to scream rather than use their emerging language.

16.6 THERAPEUTIC LANGUAGE

Talking to children with developmental delay, who also have very little language, differs in verbal content and emotional expression from talking to the child whose language is developmentally appropriate. Fewer words are used and there is more focus on the emotional intensity. It is important to take into account the child's limited understanding, as well as their lack of verbal communication. The words used need to be concrete with clear pronunciation, usually a word or short phrase associated with the immediate situation.

When attempting to talk to or negotiate with a vulnerable child, it is preferable to avoid using negative words, such as 'no', 'don't do that', 'stop that' or 'that's naughty', or threatening some punishment. With distressed children, these familiar phrases, usually used to try to produce some immediate action, can quickly lead to confrontation. It is better to try to find alternatives that acknowledge the child's distress: 'Upset boy? I can help you.' 'Those are cross hands. You need your hands for working.' 'Cross girl? You can change your feelings.' 'You came off your chair. But you're needed here.' 'Were you throwing? You need that for working.' 'I know you're upset. But you're safe with me.' If the child feels less threatened, they will be able to listen and change their behaviour.

Short sentences are used and repeated until the child understands the meaning and responds. If it is not possible to carry through what is being asked of the child, it is better not to begin, otherwise they will remain anxious and confused. The following example shows how a simple request for the child to 'sit down' was carried through to a positive conclusion. It offers guidelines only, suggesting a way of tuning in to the child, using simple language with a calm, consistent affect.

> James is a six-year-old who wants to control the situation, a familiar scenario that is fraught with fear and anxiety for the child if the adult does not set the limits. His father says, 'Please sit down.' to which James responds, 'I want to go upstairs.' His father says, 'Listen to my words, please sit down.' James responds again making other demands. His father repeats his words, 'These are Daddy's words, please sit down.' James becomes agitated, shouting to try to drown out what his father is saying, and there is a threat of impending screaming. Again his father says, 'These are Daddy's words, please sit down.' As James starts to scream in an attempt to control the situation, his father continues to use non-threatening words, repeating clearly and firmly, 'Daddy is in charge, you are not in charge, listen to my words.' James insists again with something different, but his father continues, 'Those are your words, but I want you to listen to my words,' and then adds, as James becomes quiet, 'You can use words, you don't have to scream.' The repetition of these simple words helps James to settle. He sits down, looking pleased, as if he is feeling good and not distressed as the problem has been solved.

Working within the family group provides an opportunity to support parents, and help them to facilitate their child's understanding through repetition and recognition of simple words, for example 'Mummy says', 'Daddy says', 'Sit down', 'Sit on the chair', 'Give me', 'Me', 'You', 'I', 'Mine'. And at home, everyday activities, like washing the dishes, making the beds and cooking, that are repeated every day, can be used to name simple household objects. Children whose psychological self is fragile and who have not developed the use of a pointing finger have no way of referring to themselves. By taking the child's hand, helping them to touch their chest and repeating the word 'me', it is possible to help them begin to develop a sense of self.

16.7 INTEGRATION OF LEARNING AND ■■■ LANGUAGE: CASE STUDY

The following case study, describing the initial six months of intensive therapeutic intervention with a three-year-old, illustrates how early pre-verbal learning and the establishment of the Learning Tools underpins the growth of understanding and communication.

Jonathan's father referred his son at three years old because he was not talking much. He had problems from the time he was born two weeks early after a difficult labour. He had been seen by specialists, and there was a question of brain damage and slight hearing loss. By now, both parents were in a highly anxious state and looking for guidance. He was a small, pale, rather fragile little boy with a high-pitched, squeaky voice. He breathed through his nose and dribbled. His motor coordination was poor. He did not use consonants but made a few consistent word-like sounds, which he used to try to communicate, accompanied by some gesture. Because of his limited verbal understanding and his emotional immaturity, he often screamed and cried out of sheer frustration.

In the initial Functional Learning session, Jonathan sat at the table with his mother beside him. He showed his unease by pushing the materials on the floor, slipping under the table or banging his fists and wailing. The materials were simply returned to the table and, once he settled down, it was possible to see his potential for concentrating for longer periods.

For six months, Jonathan attended for weekly sessions, sometimes with one parent, sometimes with both parents. He soon settled in to the Functional Learning activities. In the early sessions, he was given large bricks for picking up and placing in containers and, because his attention wandered, his hands were guided by his mother or father. He was helped to use alternate hands in a rhythmic way, picking up one object at a time rather than grabbing handfuls, until gradually he was able to do it by himself. Banging and scraping were introduced to increase his range of gross and fine body movements, and particularly hand–eye coordination. As he became more competent at Placing, activities using pairs of familiar common objects were used to facilitate the Pairing Tool. Pairing gradually merged into the more mature Matching with objects on a board, and then with cards, as Jonathan moved into concept work. Towards the end of the six-month period, Jonathan was given simple objects for Sorting.

In addition to the Functional Learning work, other activities were designed to address Jonathan's language needs. Articulation practice helped increase awareness of his mouth, and improve mobility and control of lips and tongue to master his consonants. Listening games were also built into the sessions, and words were linked to the various activities he enjoyed so much, such as the staircase routine where he could practice 'up' and 'down' with both parents. The parents worked with their son at home, gaining in confidence and becoming more emotionally able to understand their son's needs.

After the intensive six-month period, Jonathan was seen at regular intervals for a year, and then followed up from time to time until the age of 12. He went into a normal infant class at four and a half years old, remaining in the same school for his primary years, transferring to a secondary school which he chose himself. By then, all his learning, understanding and expressive language were age-appropriate. He remained interested in the early therapeutic work, discussing in a mature way everyday problems that had arisen at school and home since then.

(For an extended version of this case, see Stroh and Robinson, 1991.)

17

Therapeutic Work with Parents

CONTENTS

♦ A different parenting experience

♦ Responding to parents' needs

♦ Initial meeting with the family

♦ Collaborative work with parents

♦ The role of fathers

♦ Working with siblings

♦ The reluctant parent

♦ Helping parents respond to common problems

17.1 A DIFFERENT PARENTING EXPERIENCE

It is generally recognized that confident parenting in a warm, loving, secure environment provides the ideal conditions for the development of learning, communication and emotional growth of the young child. In such an environment, pleasurable responsiveness and mutual exchanges or 'intuitive parentese' (Trevarthen and Aitken, 1994) are a natural part of the young child's early experience. Of course this family environment is also available to children with developmental delay. However, the emotional reciprocity between parents and their delayed child may be late in developing with a neurologically impaired child, and may be weak and fractured with genetic, physiological, biological and psychopathological problems. These babies are not happy, contented or playful. They often cry a lot, do not sleep and may be fussy eaters. They cannot easily be comforted and do not feel secure in their environment, despite all their parents' efforts to offer the best possible care and nurturing. Parents need support and understanding, to help them make sense of this different parenting experience with a delayed child. In addition to providing the comprehensive, developmentally effective, therapeutic intervention of Functional Learning programmes, it is important to acknowledge that the needs of the parents must be synchronized with those of the child.

17.2 RESPONDING TO PARENTS' NEEDS

Trying to meet the changing needs of parents requires a delicate balance between casework, counselling and psychotherapy (Kraemer, 1987). Once they begin to participate in the Functional Learning programme, most parents develop a growing understanding of how they can work together with teachers and therapists. Working in this collaborative way, they can gradually learn how to make positive, personal adjustments to their parenting strategies and the way they respond to their child.

Therapeutic flexibility is essential when working with parents, but there is also a need for therapeutic boundaries, so that family problems can be dealt with, but primarily as they relate to the needs of the child. If it becomes clear that the child is no longer the primary focus in the Functional Learning sessions, the therapeutic boundaries will have to be redefined. Some parents acknowledge their depression and are in need of individual, personal help. Others may be overwhelmed by marital stress, making it necessary to refer them to a family counsellor or other specialist. Support for their own problems enables parents to shift the focus back to their child's needs during the learning sessions.

17.3 INITIAL MEETING WITH THE FAMILY

At the first meeting between parents and professionals, there is understandably some anxiety, and perhaps hesitancy, on both sides. Parents experience many mixed feelings about having a delayed child – shock, guilt, loss, anger, embarrassment and even revulsion. Some parents may feel panic about not being able to cope; others carry with them a sense of uncertainty after previous attempts at therapeutic intervention have not worked out. The professionals may be concerned about their own reactions to the delayed child, and whether they can express themselves sensitively enough when discussing the child with distressed parents.

17.4 COLLABORATIVE WORK WITH PARENTS

By working collaboratively with parents, professionals hope to dispel their initial hesitation. Parents, who know their child so well, are the catalyst for the transfer of information and the necessary integration of the Functional Learning work into the daily life of the family. With support, they can discover their own creativity and newfound skills in developing ideas for working with their child. When both parents are able to work together, they often develop a closer relationship as a couple, which generates greater harmony within the family, in spite of their initial unhappiness. As they watch their child's positive responses, the mutual pleasure and responsiveness felt by parents and child helps to sustain and support them, as they adjust to the new parenting strategies. As Daniel Stern (1985) puts it, 'Organizational change from within the infant and its interpretation by the parents are mutually facilitative'. Sharing the anguish as well as the positive delight, humour and laughter, as the child starts to learn and communicate, is a bonus for parents and professionals alike.

17.5 THE ROLE OF FATHERS

SHARING THE CARE OF THE DELAYED CHILD

In recent years, there has been a considerable focus on the unique and vital role that fathers play in the development of their child (Osofsky and Thompson, 2000; Pruett, 1998). It seems agreed that there are two different parenting styles, but 'both ways of being a parent can be nurturing and creative', and 'children need *both* parents' styles for optimal growth and development' (Koman and Myers, 2000).

When parents find that they have a child with developmental delay, both of them experience feelings of grief, disbelief, anxiety and stress. Neither parent has time to mourn the loss of the expected normal, 'perfect' child, as they struggle to care for and provide for the special needs of this unexpected, perhaps unresponsive and very vulnerable baby. It is as important for fathers as for mothers to participate in any therapeutic intervention, so that both parents can be supported as they try to facilitate the development of their delayed child.

But the caring role of fathers can still be marginalized. Parents do not necessarily see themselves sharing therapeutic intervention, despite, or perhaps even because of, the emotional stress and physical exhaustion of the day-to-day care of their child. Although attitudes within society have changed, and the role of the father is now generally regarded as being more than just the main earner and a support for the mother, the care of a child with special needs often reverts to the mother. Mothers often feel they carry the guilt of having this different child, adding to their determination to take on the role of main caregiver. The father feels pushed aside but, though angry, does not want to be emotionally in competition with his partner. In trying to keep the peace, he may lose confidence about participating more directly in the daily care of his child, falling back on the traditional role of being the disciplinarian and family breadwinner.

■ PARTICIPATION IN THERAPEUTIC INTERVENTION

For practitioners whose therapeutic focus is helping the child, it can be easy to accept that fathers do not need to share in the care of their delayed child, and so they may not recognize the benefits of the father being a second carer, and participating in the therapy programme along with the mother. But it is an emotional loss to both parents and child if the fathering role is not encouraged. Fathers contribute a different though complementary nurturing role to mothers. They can hug, kiss, feed, talk to, carry, swing, bath, change and toilet their child, and they are able to physically contain their child during periods of stress or outbursts of immature rage. A secure attachment to the father leads to a confident and competent child, who is better adapted to relating to other people, and more likely to develop a wider range of interactive skills.

Once fathers are encouraged to contribute fully to looking after their child, and understand the importance of their role, they are usually delighted to share in the therapeutic intervention, making time for regular clinic visits and taking part in activities with their child at home. One father moved his business from town to the local centre to be more available for school runs and immediate support. Another father at first thought it was 'sinister' to be asked to share the care of his son but, once he understood the importance of his fathering role, he took a year out to be the principal carer when his wife was depressed, finding original and imaginative ways of helping his son.

17.6 WORKING WITH SIBLINGS

When working with families, it can be beneficial to see other carers or family members, like grandparents, who may be sharing the child's care. It is particularly important to take into account the emotional needs of siblings, many of whom have their own anxieties about their brother or sister, and feel a certain amount of anger and jealousy about the amount of time their parents seem to spend with them. Family group meetings can be used to encourage them to express their feelings, however ambivalent. This often gives parents an insight into the needs of their other children, and they can make changes and adjust the family balance, if necessary, to support and reassure them. Sometimes it is possible for a sibling to join a Functional Learning session, where they can see their brother or sister learning and responding to work which, in the case of an older sibling, they recognize, often with surprise, is similar to the work they do in school.

17.7 THE RELUCTANT PARENT

Therapists have to accept that not all parents feel able to take part in the work with their delayed child. There are parents who are ambivalent about it or who prefer the professional to do the work with the child. There are others who find that they do not agree with the kind of intervention being offered. Their fears and anxieties may be so overwhelming that they are not able to listen and take in any information being given to them. For example, a three-year-old autistic boy found all change intolerable. His outbursts of crying and screaming when confronted by any change controlled both parents. But his mother did not see it this way; she thought of this behaviour as 'knowing his own mind'. She did not find it possible to work in collaboration, because she saw the basic idea of helping her child to sit on a chair until he settled as 'interfering with his freedom'. He was already a large, powerful child, so both parents were needed to contain him. The father was less ambivalent than the mother but he sided with her, not wanting to arouse anger or discontent between them. It was not possible to overcome the fears and anxieties of these parents, and there was a mutual agreement that Functional Learning was not compatible with what they wanted for their son.

17.8 HELPING PARENTS RESPOND TO COMMON PROBLEMS

When parents seek help for their child whose development is delayed, they usually describe problems in a number of different areas of behaviour and everyday activities, most commonly, sleeping, eating and playing. Very often, these problems had begun to show themselves in the early months of the infant's development. Functional Learning seeks to offer an integrative programme, both to facilitate the early Learning Tools and to help with these other aspects of development. As parents gradually begin to understand the special difficulties of their delayed child, they can begin to respond more appropriately, learning new caring strategies that lower tensions and anxieties within the family.

ESTABLISHING A REGULAR SLEEP PATTERN

Sleep is vitally important for both infant and parents. It allows the child to rest and gives the parents, often exhausted from being with their child most of the day, an opportunity to have time away from their child and share time together as a couple. A good sleeping pattern for all children is when the child consistently settles to sleep soon after being put to bed. This kind of regular sleeping pattern is not easy to establish for children with developmental delay, who often have difficulty in going to sleep or staying asleep.

Of course the situation is different for every child and family but there are some commonly occurring problems. There are the children who cannot be comforted and only go to sleep when they are carried for long periods by their parents. There are others whose sensitivity makes it almost impossible to put them down, even once they are asleep, as the slightest change in position arouses anxiety and crying. Some children repeatedly get out of bed and need to be put back, while others leave their own bed to go into their parents' room, demanding to share their bed.

But parents can be supported to use consistent strategies to try to establish a regular sleep pattern for their child. Some strategies can have an immediate effect, but others may take weeks or months before they become routine and are eventually understood by the child, with good results. Simplicity, calmness and emotional continuity are essential for both child and parents. Parents learn that they need to be united in their efforts to help get their child to sleep, knowing there will be a shared pleasurable outcome for both them and their child once a good sleep pattern is established.

There are a number of basic principles underpinning attempts to help parents establish a sleep routine. Every child needs to understand that a bed is a place for sleeping and that they need to sleep in their *own* bed. If another sleeping place is offered, say the parents' bed, this choice either confuses the child or could overload the child's limited understanding. It is important to have a regular and consistent time for the child to go to bed. Parents need to maintain an emotional calm, and to approach the bedtime routine without anger or pleading. Once the child is in bed, parents can perhaps read a story or sing, and then leave them tucked up in bed. If the child cries, one parent returns to settle them, while the other parent continues with what they are doing. If the child does not settle once the parent leaves the room, after two or three attempts, the parent remains in the room sitting in a comfortable chair or lying on the floor, until the child is asleep. This procedure may need to continue over many nights, weeks or even months. Parents can alternate, one of them staying with the child while their partner looks after other children, or has time to eat and sleep. Once Functional Learning activities are established and children begin to work with effort and understanding, there is often a spin-off and they settle and sleep better.

MEALTIMES

Developmental delay in young children is often associated with difficult feeding behaviour, resulting in constant frustration for parents. Food is usually an anticipated pleasurable experience, but having a child who does not respond positively can mean that mealtimes become a nightmare. As parents become increasingly frustrated, they resort to cajoling, bribery and anger. Home visiting in conjunction with a feeding programme, described in 18.5, can have a positive therapeutic outcome. During the mealtimes at home, it is possible to offer positive strategies which can have an immediate effect. Sometimes only small changes are needed to help overcome certain unsuccessful responses, allowing parent and child to begin to share the kind of pleasure and enjoyment that is usually part of the normal feeding experience. If the parents are willing, it can be useful to make a recording of the mealtime which parents and practitioner can view together. Parents can then see for themselves the positive changes they were able to make, perhaps in spite of the inner turmoil they may have felt.

PLAY

Many children with developmental delay do not play spontaneously. Sometimes it can be helpful to observe the child and parents together, to be able to discuss the child's responses, and to support the parents as they begin to help their child develop early play.

Parents of a three-year-old diagnosed as being on the autistic spectrum were bewildered by his behaviour and his lack of exploration. The only object he showed any interest in was a toy car that he pushed back and forth endlessly without looking at it. Any attempt by either parent to intervene resulted in anger, screaming and rejection, which added to their feelings of inadequacy and so they usually withdrew.

Supporting their presence during the playtime and talking them through their son's obsessive movement and negative responses helped them to understand that this was part of his overall developmental delay. All change felt catastrophic to this little boy and, to protect himself, he developed secondary defensive behaviours – the retreat, the screaming and the obsessive behaviours. With this new understanding, the parents were better able to tolerate their son's responses as well as becoming aware of their own emotional sensitivity. They slowly made positive changes in their own responses, keeping eye contact and physical contact to a minimum, using single, affective words and staying with him on the floor, until eventually he began to tolerate their presence.

His screaming stopped and he made small, timid changes in the way he responded, touching other objects and even beginning to acknowledge his parents. As they increased their spontaneity and liveliness his level of activity also increased. Soon there were smiles of delight, babbling and playful movements, until eventually there was a to and fro between the parents and their son, who started to move towards them when they called his name. At the same time, in the Functional Learning sessions, the parents were helping their son with picking up and placing activities. As his curiosity and self-motivation slowly grew, they were able to find opportunities to extend this simple activity into the playtime at home, until eventually play became a pleasurable and shared experience.

18

Feeding and Eating in Young Children with Developmental Delay

---

CONTENTS

◆ Feeding as a therapeutic tool

◆ Early infant feeding

◆ Feeding as a diagnostic tool

◆ Primary and secondary feeding problems

◆ Establishing a good feeding experience

◆ Feeding can be part of therapeutic intervention: a case study

---

18.1 FEEDING AS A THERAPEUTIC TOOL

The use of feeding as a therapeutic tool goes back to the early work at High Wick Hospital (Stroh, Robinson and Stroh, 1986). Since then, there has been an explosion of interest in feeding problems and the development of feeding programmes as a part of therapeutic intervention. Speech and language therapists undertake special training in how to support the development of eating and drinking in children with conditions such as cerebral palsy or gastro-oesophageal reflux (Winstock, 2005). Popular television programmes focusing on family dysfunction offer guidance for helping young children with severe feeding problems. There is a wealth of information on the Internet offering guidelines to parents/carers concerned about their child's feeding difficulties. The importance of feeding cannot be overestimated, though it may often be taken for granted, like breathing. Successful feeding can provide therapeutic opportunities for increased trust, shared pleasure and emotional awareness as well as a potential for learning, communicating and understanding between parents and their child.

18.2 EARLY INFANT FEEDING

Feeding represents the earliest interaction – between the child and feeder, from birth – and it is associated with the first intimate relationship. Food is the earliest intrusion that is brought to the child from the environment (Kanner, 1973). It is the basis of judgement, the beginning of sorting out – if it is good or bad, whether to eat it or spit it out (Freud, 1925). Early pleasurable feeding leads to trust. Taking in food is also the most consistently repetitive interaction between the individual and the environment from birth. It is one essential factor in the child's development of autonomy, a sense of being a separate person – choosing whether or not to eat and what food to eat. Eating changes discomfort into comfort. It is the prototype of 'taking things in', of internalization, and the basis for the development of early communication.

18.3 FEEDING AS A DIAGNOSTIC TOOL

Feeding behaviour is a fundamental element in any comprehensive developmental profile of the young delayed child. Looking systematically at the earliest feeding experiences can provide a sensitive diagnostic tool. Feeding behaviour can reflect the child's preferred style of adjustment to the environment – whether they are curious, hesitant, needing support, or happy to try anything new. It can indicate events in the early history, which may help to explain the depth, or apparent absence, of strong emotions in the child. It can also provide information about important aspects of the parent/child relationship.

18.4 PRIMARY AND SECONDARY FEEDING PROBLEMS

Many infants and children with developmental delay have feeding problems of greater or lesser severity, though some may be disguised or not regarded as significant. Developmentally, from birth, eating is or becomes unpleasurable. Instead of turning discomfort into comfort, feeding increases discomfort. Eating becomes a threatening experience, leading to the fundamental conflict between the basic need to eat and the intense fear of doing so.

Loving parents, who have tried to feed and nurture their delayed child, often end up feeling inadequate if their child is not eating well even after all their attempts. They may have tried all sorts of strategies, including diverting the child with games or books, offering bribes, insisting on the child eating, withdrawing their love or resorting to anger, or a mixture of all of these, to try to overcome the control of the child who is refusing to eat or will only eat certain foods. They are often cautious when describing feeding and mealtimes, and dread the feeling of guilt, as they are sure they will be judged to be incompetent.

PRIMARY FEEDING PROBLEMS

There are many causes of early feeding difficulties. Premature babies may not have a strong sucking reflex and take longer to become strong enough to suck vigorously. There are studies of deprived babies in orphanages left to feed themselves with the bottle propped up on a cushion. These infants have been observed to suck a little, then hold the milk in their cheeks for long periods, gradually letting it out into their mouths and swallowing – giving themselves comfort over time. Autistic children do not make early visual or tactile contact with breast or bottle, so food is felt as intrusive and not eaten with pleasure. This lack of contact precludes any close emotional links with the feeder. Children with poor coordination, because of delayed neuromotor development, can be difficult to feed.

SECONDARY FEEDING PROBLEMS

There are many problem feeding behaviours that children develop in response to primary feeding difficulties, to try to overcome their feelings of displeasure and the anxiety and tensions surrounding the taking in of food. Some examples are:

- 'non-eating eating' – automatic, mechanical eating with little pleasure or awareness
- shovelling in large amounts of food, gulping food
- avoidance of touching food with the lips, pushing the spoon/hand away
- spitting or regurgitation
- excessive turning away and screaming
- throwing food
- refusing to sit on the chair
- scavenging – taking food from other plates
- excessive food fads – refusal to eat anything other than preferred food
- holding food in the mouth for long periods without swallowing
- patterning – modifying or playing with the food in various ways, only eating it after changing the way it looks and feels.

18.5 ESTABLISHING A GOOD FEEDING
EXPERIENCE

Establishing a good feeding experience can be a very successful way for parents/carers to develop intimacy and pleasurable contact with the child who is developmentally delayed. Individual, one-to-one mealtimes can be set up by parents/carers, away from the noise and distractions of family meals, and the child can be given small portions of simple food on a spoon.

FEEDING PROCEDURE

- The preferred setting is a quiet, settled environment where you can sit together with the child, undisturbed.

- Ideally, you need to have this special, individual mealtime with the child for all meals, but if this is not possible, it should be done for at least one meal a day.

- The type of food needs to be carefully considered and you only need small amounts. Plain, simple food is preferable, such as mashed potato, fish fingers, or soft fruit, or start with the child's preferred food.

- Offer small amounts of food on a spoon, and wait for the child to take it from the spoon. At this stage, you keep the spoon; the child does not have a spoon or use it themselves.

- To start with, there may be no response or the child may push the spoon away and turn away. Simply return the spoon to rest on the plate, then try again, calmly and slowly.

- End the meal after 20 minutes, accepting without comment whatever amount the child has eaten, and leave the table with the child.

- During the mealtime, it is better to keep verbal interaction to a minimum to ensure that talking does not become a distraction. Anything that is said should be about the food and being together.

- Try to be as quiet and relaxed as possible, with a calm facial expression when offering the food to the child, allowing the child to decide when to eat it. Then there is no need for cajoling or persuasion.

- Try to ensure that there is some contact or visual awareness, even if only minimal, between you and the child before the food is eaten.

- It is not helpful for the child to be tricked into eating, for example by saying 'open your mouth' and quickly putting the spoon in, or pretending to fly a plane around the child's head, then spooning in the food when the child is not looking, or singing nursery rhymes as a distraction. All of this is confusing to a worried and fearful child. The aim is to help the child take in food with awareness and pleasure.

Once the child begins to eat small amounts of food from the spoon, some variations can be introduced, provided they are slowly, carefully and sensitively timed. The child who is beginning to accept food can occasionally be given the spoon, or at the end of the meal you can offer the child something like a few pieces of fruit. Eventually, you and the child can take turns putting the food on the spoon and you can scrape the plate together. Gradually you can increase the amount and variety of food. But you still need to give the child only small amounts of food at a time, which provides an opportunity to use simple language, such as asking for 'more'. You can model this normal communication, repeating it when the child attempts the sound, just as you would with any young child beginning to talk. Naming the food can also help to build up a vocabulary around the pleasure now associated with food.

FAMILY MEALTIMES

When a more normal eating pattern begins to emerge and food becomes pleasurable, the child can rejoin the rest of the family for some mealtimes. But you still need to give them only small portions of food, and if there are any signs of stress it is important to return to an individual one-to-one mealtime. As the child continues to settle, they can be encouraged to take part in the food preparation, choosing the amount they want and taking responsibility for setting the table.

There will be ups and downs for some time, reflecting how the child functions within the family, so it is a good idea to try to keep all mealtimes as calm and quiet as possible. Parents/carers need to be flexible, being prepared to try different arrangements according to the needs of the child. For example, one parent can have breakfast with the child before the rest of the family appears. This quiet, individual time gives the child a chance to be involved in making choices, helping to prepare the food and sharing the experience with the parent.

18.6 FEEDING CAN BE PART OF THERAPEUTIC INTERVENTION: A CASE STUDY

This account illustrates how a family can be helped to establish a good feeding experience for their child, as part of an integrated therapeutic intervention.

Initial interview

Jack was referred when he was four-and-a-half years old with long-standing feeding difficulties. A normal eating pattern had never been established, despite two attempts at intervention, and he would still only eat baby food. The initial session with Jack and his family soon made it clear that there were other developmental problems. Jack talked a lot and tried to make jokes but his language was immature. He was not yet dressing or undressing himself and he was still bed-wetting.

In order to keep any anxiety to a minimum, Jack was not formally assessed at this first meeting but given a range of early learning activities. Although his early Learning Tools were established – he could place, pair, match, sort, sequence and draw – his level of ability in these activities was not what one would expect of a four-and-a-half year old. There was a basic inflexibility in the way he did things that interfered with and held up his learning. His behaviour was immature, he had difficulty in sitting still, he tried to move away from the table and hide, and his chatter disrupted his concentration.

The family

There was resentment and hostility from both parents when the idea of a feeding programme for Jack was discussed with them, as they had tried other programmes that had been disastrous. But they were in agreement that Jack needed some help with his learning before starting school, and they accepted the planned Functional Learning activities. Jack's brother did not want Jack to go to his school, because he found his behaviour embarrassing, and he thought the other children would make fun of Jack as he did not eat 'proper food'. It turned out that none of the family members had pleasurable eating expectations or experiences, and the general non-integration of the family was reflected in their eating habits.

Early feeding experience

Jack was a full-term baby and was bottle-fed. Twice in his first six months he was hospitalized, creating a very distressing time for his parents who had to try to feed him with the necessary medication. At two years, just as his parents were beginning to help him to use a spoon, they had to deal with other family problems and were unable to support Jack, leaving him to feed himself. Consequently, normal feeding was never established.

Feeding behaviour

Jack ate only baby cereal and one kind of yoghurt. He sometimes used a spoon to feed himself, but otherwise was spoon-fed. He drank mainly water. Mealtimes had become a battleground, with Jack's parents resorting to tricking and deception. They had even tried withholding Jack's preferred food, but when he held out they gave in. As the parents and Jack were locked inexorably together, with Jack having the final control, any change in Jack would need to be accompanied by changes in both parents.

Planned intervention

The comprehensive therapeutic intervention aimed to facilitate all the necessary changes for Jack and his family. It was designed to establish pleasurable feeding behaviour, lessening Jack's fears and anxiety surrounding food, and offering opportunities for the parents to learn new strategies to help him. Functional Learning activities would aim to strengthen Jack's Learning Tools, generally extending his learning experiences, improving concentration and attention, and enabling him to move on to early reading and writing activities. Some family group time would be built into the sessions, to initiate discussion concerning Jack's place within the family and how he felt about himself.

Because the family lived at a distance, therapeutic sessions were limited to ten two-hour sessions over three months. The whole family, including Jack's older brother, were involved in the therapy and came at regular intervals in various combinations. Each of the parents had special mealtimes with Jack at home.

Learning activities

Jack settled and started to enjoy the activities he was given. They were all within his level of competence, so he did not fail and always wanted to do more. A natural outcome of his success was an improvement in his concentration and attention span. His Learning Tools were consolidated and extended, and his problem-solving strategies became less rigid and more diversified.

The sessions with Jack were also used to help him express his fears and fantasies through his drawings. He used his drawings of monsters to describe his feelings about himself and how he thought of himself in his family. He started using appropriate language to express these feelings – his sadness and anger, his fears of eating and hostility to change. He began to understand how difficult it was for him to pretend to be so powerful when he was only a little boy.

On several occasions, Jack's brother shared part of the session, usually sitting at a separate table, drawing or working at some other activity he had brought. He was very aware of his brother's newfound abilities, and was relieved that Jack was not 'thick', as he had feared. He was both jealous and resentful of all the time his parents were now spending with Jack, but he was also very caring of his younger brother. Both children were helped to share their feelings about each other and the changes that were taking place within the family.

The feeding programme

It was agreed that a short feeding session would occasionally be part of the therapeutic time and this would be videoed. The special daily mealtimes at home with Jack would be done in a similar way. To fit in with their work and other family commitments, Jack's father helped him at breakfast and the evening meal, and his mother was with him for lunch.

The environment was to be settled and quiet, with Jack sitting at the table with either his mother or his father, so that he had a one-to-one feeding experience, with a slow, sensitive weaning towards other foods. These new foods would be other cereals, similar in texture and taste to his preferred baby cereal. Jack's parents were to avoid insisting, cajoling, pleading or getting angry. The new food would be seen and understood by Jack, not 'hidden' as in the past. The baby cereal would be mixed with a tiny piece of another cereal that they had in the house. Jack would put his preferred food on his plate, and then take some of the other cereal, mixing both of them himself. Initially, he

(Continued)

(Continued)

was hesitant and could not mix the cereals with water or milk, so ate them dry. Gradually, every meal was slightly altered, with Jack adding a tiny amount of the new food before feeding himself.

Therapeutic time with parents

Dealing with the emotional, marital and parenting problems of Jack's parents was as important as trying to help Jack. Working with them was not a comfortable and accepting experience. They were angry about being referred for therapy, partly because of the previous unsuccessful treatment programme. Their ambivalence was evident in their initial difficulty in keeping their appointment, despite the time being changed to try to accommodate them.

But giving them time for themselves, focusing on their own feelings and life problems, allowed them to work through their anger and ambivalence. They were able to talk more about their differences, their own needs and the changes that were taking place every day at mealtimes. They gradually understood that they needed to make emotional adjustments themselves, to synchronize with the changes in Jack. As their confidence and competence began to return, they became more flexible and began to enjoy having meals with both their children.

Mealtimes with parents: development of normal eating

Jack's parents initially struggled to make the changes in the mealtimes, both finding it an emotionally draining experience. Although they carried out the new routine during mealtimes with Jack, it took two months before they really understood the importance of offering food in this way. As their feelings became more positive, and they became more sensitive to Jack's cues, they were able to give him a wider variety of food. They always used the same procedure, adding new food in small portions to the preferred food. Although they did find Jack's continuing protests irritating, they no longer responded with anger, remaining quietly in control. As Jack improved, both parents used their own creativity to help him extend his choice and preparation of food. On one occasion, when Jack saw some brown pieces in the cereal he had put in the bowl himself, he asked his father if they were 'brown stones'. His father understood Jack was worried, and said matter-of-factly that they were part of the cereal. Jack ate the cereal without further anxiety, reflecting his newfound trust.

At first, Jack's mother found the lunchtime meal difficult because she felt Jack was being provocative. She had the idea of keeping a diary of the mealtimes to follow his progress. It helped her to tolerate Jack's controlling behaviour, and his need to have her close to him while he was eating, if she wrote it down afterwards. She also began to understand Jack's emotional need to be close, once she was able to make links to her unsatisfactory experiences and fears when trying to feed Jack as a baby and finding it difficult to feel close to him.

From eating different cereals, Jack extended his range to eating small pieces of toast that he could cut and butter. Eventually, he began to eat vegetables and soup, which he prepared and cooked for himself at lunchtimes with his mother, and then even baked beans. He enjoyed the mealtimes with both parents. Once he could manage baked beans at home, he was able to eat with his friends and ask for baked beans and yoghurt.

Final outcome

Before Jack started primary school, a school visit was arranged to meet his future teacher to talk about his emotional sensitivity, the feeding progress and the Functional Learning programme. By then, he had been formally assessed, showing an age-appropriate level of non-verbal ability.

From his first day at school, Jack was able to take his lunch and eat it with the other children. His learning progressed and he kept up with his peer group. His ability to amuse others was successfully adapted to acting in the school plays. Jack and his mother attended for a follow-up session nine months later, when he ate a sandwich lunch they had prepared together at home and brought with them.

SECTION V

FUNCTIONAL LEARNING IN DIFFERENT SETTINGS

Section V demonstrates the potential for using Functional Learning to support children in different educational environments cross-culturally. It provides a model for setting up Functional Learning workshops.

19

A Class in a Residential Unit

CONTENTS

♦ The Learning Tools – into normal education

♦ Integration of Learning Tools

♦ Other learning activities

19.1 THE LEARNING TOOLS – INTO NORMAL EDUCATION

RESEARCH AND DEVELOPMENT

The research and development of Functional Learning and the Learning Tools, at High Wick, arose out of the association with Geoffrey Waldon and his ideas about early learning (see 1.3). It was based on observation of the normal development of young children, which showed that Learning Tools were an integral part of children's play. It is not so hard to see that the learning that emerged from this early exploration and play was learning for daily living. Perhaps not as clear is how the Learning Tools prepare children to understand and deal with educational activities in school. This account, based on the work the children did, and the way they were supported in what was known as the 'school group' at High Wick – geared towards normal education while retaining Functional Learning principles – shows how this can be done. There were usually five or six children in the group, in the 8–12-year age range, all of whom had learning, behaviour and emotional problems. A question asked by one of the children – 'Why do I find it so easy now when I used to find it so difficult?' – reflected the successful experience of learning to learn provided by Functional Learning.

SCHOOL ENVIRONMENT

Just as in setting up Functional Learning sessions it is important to reduce the 'noise' or visual distraction that the child has to cope with, the same applied to the school group classroom. Learning materials and other equipment were kept at the back of the room behind the children, who faced a more or less plain, empty wall and the teacher's table. Pictures on walls and other objects around the room were kept to a minimum. Each child had their own desk, but they certainly saw themselves as part of a group. This awareness was reinforced by group learning sessions in addition to individual work. Desks were kept clear, apart from the work the child had to deal with at the time. The teacher and childcare assistants working with the children kept language to a minimum, and as far as possible related to what they were doing. Social interaction was kept to break/play times. This is not unlike what we all do at times when we need to concentrate. Universities provide libraries where a student can work in quiet surroundings. Even at home we ask for 'quiet' when attempting a difficult problem in a crossword or complicated knitting.

GROUP WORK

The children needed to learn to work in groups, to be aware of and take into account what the others in the group were doing. Members of a group are often at different levels of understanding. In everyday life, in situations where some are in training and still learning, and others are more knowledgeable, work is shared appropriately between them. The same principle was used with the children, which meant of course knowing each child's ability, so that the activity could be divided into appropriate task levels among the children in the group. Where the children are all at the same level of understanding, of course greater flexibility within the task is possible.

19.2 INTEGRATION OF LEARNING TOOLS

The Learning Tools have been described individually in Section II so that they can be more easily understood. But, in reality, they overlap and combine during the child's early development, and this is even more apparent later on in activities at home and in school. Just as, in everyday life, the Learning Tools are combined to perform a variety of tasks, the same was true for the children's activities, such as cooking, pottery and shopping. It was important to identify the Learning Tools involved in these more general activities, so a simple chart was designed on which the child's activity could be briefly described and the Learning Tools involved could be 'box-ticked'.

PLACING AND PILING

Flexibility of thinking and the ability to make appropriate choices are key elements of Functional Learning. Placing and Piling are both acceptable ways of moving objects from one place to another. But while dirty clothes can be piled into a clothes basket, dirty dishes would not be piled into a dishwasher, but rather need to be placed with some care. The child's understanding of these different objects and materials is based on mature Sorting. Placing becomes even more sophisticated, for example, in maths, placing a number one in a different column changes it from a one to a ten.

BANGING AND DRAWING

Banging and scraping lead to the use of tools like crayons or pencils for drawing. This Learning Tool needs to be well developed to enable the child to do written work (see 15.5). Activities such as pottery and simple woodwork or other handicrafts extend the child's ability to use tools, which needs to be linked to competent Placing, Sorting and Sequencing.

PAIRING AND MATCHING

Through Pairing and Matching, the child looks at similarities and differences, in order to bring together two objects or cards that 'belong' together. In Matching, the complexity of this 'belonging together' increases, and can even be by association only, such as hat and coat, knife and fork, pencil and paper, tree and leaves, and eventually a word that goes with an object or picture.

SORTING

When the child can sort five sets and understands Sorting by concepts like furniture, people, animals, transport, clothing, utensils, or buildings, the use of Sorting and the thinking involved is quite complicated. Objects can be looked at in terms of various aspects, like colour, shape, texture, size, material, use, or location. These are all possible criteria for sorting things and indicate that thinking has become a kind of network of ideas. The material wood, for example, can be linked to trees, carpentry, wooden furniture, boats and houses old and new.

GROUP SORTING

To help children understand and accept that there are different ways of looking at objects, Sorting can be done as a group activity. A group of four children is given a container full of objects and some other containers to sort them into. The number of sets the objects will be sorted into can either be pre-determined or, if the children have the necessary understanding, they can be left to decide for themselves. The children take it in turns to take an object from the container and decide how to sort it. The rule that they can change around objects sorted by other children will depend on the level of frustration it is felt the children can cope with. They learn to recognize how objects are perceived by others and come to a group decision. The early Functional Learning experience, which has kept the introduction of language to a minimum and related it to the task in hand, helps keep the children's language focused at this stage. Cards that can be sorted in different ways can also be used for this group activity.

THEORY OF SETS

Once children understand that objects and information can be sorted into various categories, according to the way we look at them, they can see that an object can belong to at least two categories simultaneously. They are ready to work with sets and the intersection involved in the early theory of sets. Up to now, objects have been sorted into containers and cards onto boards, but at this point hoops can be used. Each hoop contains a set, and the hoops can be overlapped to form the intersection of two sets, creating a Venn diagram. Children who can draw can use Venn diagrams to illustrate the sets. Of course this is a familiar educational activity, but Functional Learning helps to understand the thinking necessary to be able to do the activity. The children have come to the theory of sets by slow stages, stretching the boundaries of their learning all the time, with each new stage or body of new understanding being on the periphery of the understanding they already had.

SEQUENCING

TIME

Sequencing governs our daily lives. The time sequence measured by hours, days, weeks and years allows us to project into the future with our plans and anticipate coming events. Children can experience this future time by ticking off days on a calendar as an event draws near. History is looking back along the time sequence. For most children, the period they look back on is fairly short. An activity such as drawing a picture of a past holiday while looking forward to a future one, helps children experience the sequence of time in real everyday terms they can understand. If they want to measure time in hours, it is easier on a digital clock where only increasing numbers are involved.

NUMBER

Sequencing can be used to explore number. For example, objects and containers can be used to illustrate increasing and decreasing quantity. A row of five shallow containers, each with five small objects, is placed in front of the child. Below and in line with the first row of containers is a second row of five empty containers. The child moves along the row in sequence, taking one object from the first container and placing it in the empty container below. Two objects are taken from the second container, three from the third and so on along the row. In the top row of containers, there is now a decreasing number of objects, and in the row of containers below an increasing number of objects, as Figure 51 shows. A great deal of number work is about recognizing pattern, and using objects like this helps the child to see the pattern.

The child can draw the containers and, in a square below each one, they can write the number representing the number of objects. The relationship between

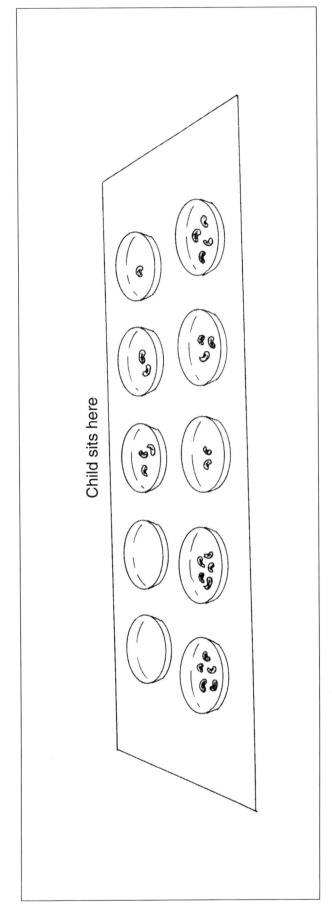

Child sits here

FIGURE 51 NUMBER SEQUENCING USING OBJECTS.

addition and subtraction can be explored, using either the containers with objects or the child's drawing. This brings together a sequence of size or quantity with a code – a number – used to indicate quantity. There are of course other codes for size, weight, distance, etc. which also relate to a sequence.

It is very important for children to use concrete materials like this to develop an understanding of number, rather than simply carrying out number operations using abstract symbols. Functional Learning provides children with activities for exploring objects to develop their early Learning Tools, providing a foundation of understanding for later learning of abstract concepts. Montessori materials also help children learn through their senses, so that abstract number concepts are introduced through concrete materials (Lillard, 2007). Another example is the maths scheme, *Mathematics Their Way* (Baratta-Lorton, 1998), which provides extensive activities and ideas to help children learn about number concepts by exploring real materials.

SEQUENCE OF EVENTS

Events can either be complex, like mealtimes during the day, or the small events that make up a single activity. Once the child has used cards that illustrate the sequence of events involved in making a cup of tea, they can make their own simple drawings. They need to be given the opportunity to talk through the sequence, to help them rethink areas where their drawing of the sequence of events might be unclear.

FILLING THE GAPS

Sometimes there are gaps in sequences – where there is something missing. The child needs to understand the logic of the sequence so that they can fill in any gaps. This can be done initially with very simple sequences using objects or cards, and then extended so that the child draws in what is missing. A repeating sequence is the easiest sequence to use for filling in gaps, for example a series of coloured squares – red, blue, yellow – repeated, but with the occasional blank square which the child fills in. An expansive sequence, for example a glass being filled with liquid from a jug so that, as the jug empties, the glass fills, requires an understanding of what is happening for the child to work out any gaps in the sequence.

BRICK BUILDING

The Brick Building Tool helps the child to develop spatial awareness, and to understand how shapes can be put together to create a 'model'. This learning can now be used to help the child move into writing and reading.

MODELS

As an extension of Brick Building, the child creates a three-dimensional model from a two-dimensional plan. This ability can be used in activities such as woodwork when something is made by following a plan. An example of this in everyday life is putting together flat-pack furniture, something many of us have struggled with.

WRITING

Writing is a series of shapes put together to form a letter, the equivalent of the 'model' in Brick Building. Putting these shapes together requires not only fine motor control but also spatial awareness. An uppercase 'H' is created by drawing the two uprights first, then joining them together with the cross piece. The child uses the kind of understanding developed through Brick Building to create the letter 'H'. A series of such shapes (letters), for example 'h', 'a', 't', grouped together, form a word, 'hat'. These letters also represent, or form a code, for a group of sounds. The child needs to be able to sequence to put the sounds together for reading.

READING

In putting together the code of shapes/sounds in a sequence, we are reading. Each word is of course a code – it represents an object, an activity, a concept, etc. Not everyone writes the letters in exactly the same way, and they may differ considerably in print. The experience of Matching will help the child understand these differences. Eventually, when the Learning Tools involved in writing and reading are firmly established, writing and reading themselves can become tools for further learning and communication.

19.3 OTHER LEARNING ACTIVITIES

TRAFFIC COUNT

During the early stages of Functional Learning, the child feels safe seated at a table. Gradually, the child moves away from the table to work on the floor, around the room and even moving between two rooms. Eventually, activities can take place outside, where the security of the table is left behind and there are more possible distractions. Many different ways of practising all the Learning Tools outside can be explored and developed.

An activity such as a traffic count not only moves the activity of Sorting out of doors, but moves it very much into everyday life. Sorting transport according to different criteria can be done with cards first, before the child is ready to face the real thing. Cars, lorries, buses and bikes are all part of transport but are also different. In order to record the findings, the child needs to be able to use a pencil. A chart of some sort can be designed to record the findings, which requires an understanding of Coding. For the count to be a meaningful experience, the child needs to have an understanding of increasing quantities/numbers, as well as the code we use to represent number. The acquisition of the Learning Tools, and the combining of those tools to solve a problem, make possible a simple activity like a traffic count.

COOKING

Cooking is a tremendously useful activity, because it involves so many of the Learning Tools, and most children like to make food for themselves. To start with, recipes can be shown as a series of pictures. To be able to use these recipe cards, the child has to be able to translate a two-dimensional picture into three-dimensional objects, one of the Brick Building activities. Sequencing is required to understand the information on the cards and to add the ingredients in the right order. Sorting is necessary to choose the ingredients needed from the store cupboard. The ability to use tools, developed from Banging and Scraping, is needed for mixing and cutting. Being able to place in even more complex ways is essential. An important feature of cooking is the transformation of the ingredients from a raw state to a cooked state. Children do not always understand this change, which can contribute to the difficulties children with developmental delay have with eating. Sometimes simple food, such as cheese on toast, where the child can watch the transformation under the grill, is helpful. As children move to more complex cooking and start to read simple recipes, they are using both Coding and Sequencing.

SHOPPING

Shopping can be a useful learning experience, but some of the activities involved in shopping can be practised first in a familiar, contained environment, before venturing into the highly distracting environment of a shop or supermarket. For example the complexities of using money can be explored. This involves Coding, where each coin or note represents or stands for an amount of money, and Sorting, finding the correct coin or note from a pile of money. The kind of communications needed for carrying out transactions when shopping can also be practised. One way to do this is to run a small, weekly tuck shop, where the children not only purchase things but also serve, with the support of an adult.

Children need to be able to sort and code to choose things they want to buy. They need to match and pair if they want to buy something they have bought before. Placing plays a big part in shopping, particularly in supermarkets. Goods are taken from the shelf and placed in the trolley; taken from the trolley and placed on the counter; and placed into bags after payment. The bags are then placed back in the trolley. From the trolley the bags are placed usually into a car. At home the goods are taken out of the bags and placed into the cupboard. What we are seeing in this activity is the continuant behaviour of the young child's early Placing developed to its fullest potential. The ability to make a choice has also developed from the early decision of wanting to move an object from one place to another.

AND NOW CHILDREN CAN PROBLEM-SOLVE

In the early stages of Functional Learning, children who have previously often experienced failure may try to keep everything the same, out of fear of the unknown. Now the Learning Tools are developed enough to enable the child to understand the environment in which life takes place. Not only can the child understand what is there, but also what is missing. The need for secondary defence behaviours is long past, and there is an ability to explore and problem-solve with confidence.

20

Functional Learning and Inclusion in Mainstream Education

CONTENTS

- Policy of inclusion

- Supporting a child in nursery and school

- How Functional Learning can facilitate learning in the classroom: a case study

20.1 POLICY OF INCLUSION

Going to nursery and then school are always milestones in a child's life. Parents often anticipate this move towards independence with some anxiety about how their child will manage. They may have concerns about which nursery or school their child will attend and the facilities that will be provided. For parents of a child with developmental problems, there is the added anxiety of deciding what kind of placement is going to be appropriate.

In the early 1980s, following the Warnock report, educational policy in the UK moved towards encouraging the inclusion of children with Special Educational Needs (SEN) in mainstream schools. The process of preparing a 'statement' was introduced to describe the needs of a child with severe difficulties and the special help required. Further legislation and guidance since then, most recently under the Special Educational Needs and Disability Act 2001, has produced a revised statutory framework regarding educational provision for SEN children. Special educational needs will be met by mainstream schools, unless parents decide they want something different for their child. Support for a child is usually provided by teaching assistants and support teachers, with a special educational needs coordinator (SENCO) responsible for SEN provision within a school.

20.2 SUPPORTING A CHILD IN NURSERY AND SCHOOL

For children who are being helped with individual Functional Learning programmes, it is beneficial for the child if the Functional Learning practitioner can liaise with the child's nursery or school. The therapist who is able to visit the child's class will be able to find out about the classroom organization and how the child fits in, as well as the learning expectations and how the child is responding. It provides an opportunity to discuss with teachers the Functional Learning work, the child's delayed learning and language, and any associated emotional and behavioural problems. Particularly if there is a support teacher working with the child, it may be possible to incorporate some of the Functional Learning activities, when appropriate, into the classroom. The Functional Learning practitioner may arrange individual sessions with the support teacher, to facilitate the continuity of the learning activities and the emotional support for the child.

20.3 HOW FUNCTIONAL LEARNING CAN FACILITATE LEARNING IN THE CLASSROOM: A CASE STUDY

This account of a child who attended a normal nursery and then a mainstream school illustrates how Functional Learning was used to facilitate learning in the classroom. This was a child on the autistic spectrum whose behaviour was challenging and whose learning and language were delayed. Although this is a description of one particular child, it can be used as a model for a collaborative approach.

Background

Tony was the second child of professional parents. Their first child was a sensitive, emotionally vulnerable boy, easily upset and often difficult to understand. Tony seemed to be a placid, undemanding baby, but at 18 months his behaviour changed. He screamed uncontrollably at every change in his environment and could not be comforted; he either completely withdrew from physical contact, turning his back or gazing out of the window, or he clung to his mother. At two years he was diagnosed as being on the autistic spectrum.

Nursery

When he was two-and-a-half years old Tony was referred for Functional Learning. There followed six months of intensive therapeutic intervention. He began to develop Learning Tools for Placing, Banging, Pairing, and Sorting and could hold a crayon for drawing. He was able to sit at a table for short periods, and to respond to simple verbal requests, and he started to relate to his parents more appropriately. At age three Tony started at the same small Montessori nursery that his brother had attended. It was agreed that his au pair would remain with him as a support helper. He went mornings only and was in a class of fewer than 20 children.

The nursery staff realized that Tony's difficult behaviour was not being 'naughty', but that he was a vulnerable, sensitive child with many fears and anxieties, and they recognized his potential for understanding and learning. There was a great deal of supportive contact between the nursery staff and the Functional Learning therapist, who visited regularly. The focus was always on finding ways to enable Tony to participate in the nursery environment, to begin to interact with the other children and to facilitate his early learning.

The children sat on their chairs first thing in the morning, but this was too worrying for Tony, so it was agreed that he would sit on the teacher's lap, until he was gradually able to accept sitting with his support helper, and then finally he was able to sit on his chair. Initially, he was not able to choose an activity from the Montessori equipment like the other children did, so materials were used that were already familiar to him from the Functional Learning sessions. He did Placing activities, such as putting shapes in holes and rings on sticks; worked with thick cards with one clear picture for Pairing, Matching and Sorting; and used thick pencils for drawing and simple joining-the-dot activities. The teachers used very simple language when talking to Tony, limiting the number of words, with everyone using the same familiar words and phrases and allowing time for him to respond.

Tony spent two years at the nursery. His previously bewildering behaviour became more predictable, so that the teachers were able to treat him more like the other children, negotiating and setting limits. His language, though not age-appropriate, had improved so that he could understand simple verbal instructions. He was able to sit with the other children, answer to his name, use the other children's names and show his daily toy at group time. He could join in activities, such as completing puzzles with a small group of a few children, although he would still occasionally hit or kick another child.

Primary school

When he was five years old, Tony's parents decided they would like him to go to the local primary school which his brother had attended. This was a three-form entry infant school in north London, with 30 children per class. Tony had been statemented as a child with special needs, and a special learning support assistant was appointed to help him.

Initially, Tony found the noise and bustle of the classroom overwhelming, and he would put his hands over his ears. He was very difficult when he came into school in the morning. He would scream and lie on the floor, sometimes pushing and hurting the other children. His support teacher had to find ways of dealing with this behaviour which of course disrupted the class. As he still did not have much language and his understanding was limited, the language input had to be simplified. Simple words used consistently by his teachers helped to calm him and to increase his understanding – 'Tony you are safe

(Continued)

(Continued)

here.' 'We know you can work here.' 'We are all helping you in our way.' Language was also used to set limits – 'I can't allow you to hurt the other children.' 'Instead of making loud noises, use your words.' 'You are not in charge here.' He did begin to listen and respond to this therapeutic language.

Although his early learning had progressed while he was at nursery, it was still not age-appropriate, and Tony was not able to do the work that the other children were being given. It was agreed that the support teacher would provide Tony with some of the Functional Learning activities that he was familiar with, while keeping in mind the possibility of making links with classroom activities. A special workstation was set up, so that Tony could work in the classroom but have his own space. His table was positioned facing a wall, so that there was a minimum of distractions, and it was partly divided off from the rest of the room by a low bookcase. Materials for the Functional Learning activities were kept nearby. There was also a table just outside the classroom, with a few materials, where Tony could be taken to do some simple work if his behaviour was causing too much disruption, returning to the class once he was quieter. For his first year in school, the Functional Learning activities were carried out first thing every day. These were familiar activities within his level of competence, which lessened his anxiety and helped him settle, and at the same time he was learning to learn. If he got upset during the day, his support teacher would take him back to these activities at his workstation, which helped to calm him.

Tony did not find it easy to do things with the other children. But during his first year in school, his support teacher was able to help him spend short periods of time with the other children doing water play, sand play or an art activity. Playground time was a problem for him – he felt lost in the large open space, did not understand the noisy, diffuse activity and would resort to hurting the other children. His support teacher spent time in the playground with Tony by himself, showing him how to use the play equipment. After a number of weeks, she helped him to choose a couple of children to play with in a particular part of the playground, and to learn the rules of children's games, such as hide-and-seek and skipping, so that he could begin to join in.

During his second year at school, Tony was able to sit on the carpet with the other children at circle time. He would choose a carpet buddy, who would have a badge, so that he had someone to sit with him; they could help each other and he didn't have to feel lost. To help him to get used to working with other children, his support teacher would invite another child to sit with Tony at his workstation, working at something like Matching or Sorting. Once he was able to use his pointing finger, and to sequence and colour in, she also introduced worksheets appropriate to what Tony could do, so that he could see that he was doing similar work to the other children.

In addition to the work being done by the support teacher, there was a whole support network in place for those involved with helping Tony. The Functional Learning therapist made school visits from time to time. Once a term, the teachers, Functional Learning therapist and Tony's parents met to review progress. The support teacher and Functional Learning therapist met frequently to monitor the programme that was being carried out in school, based on Functional Learning activities to support the growth of Tony's Learning Tools.

At the end of the second year, Tony moved into the next class with his school group. He had a different support teacher but he settled down well. He got up in the morning and got ready for school. He went straight into the playground, lined up and went into the classroom with the other children. He was able to settle on the mat for discussion time. He followed through all the classroom activities. There was very little difficulty with behaviour. He listened to stories and would join in question-and-answer time with the other children round the table. He joined PE and assembly. In the playground, he joined in with the other children – he understood the rules of games, took his turn and did not hit the other children. He was fully integrated into the structure of the day.

21

International Links

CONTENTS

- ◆ Learning Tools are cross-cultural

- ◆ Hanover, Germany – special education unit

- ◆ Nicosia, Cyprus – individual Functional Learning programmes

- ◆ Slovenia – Functional Learning training programmes

- ◆ A Functional Learning workshop programme

- ◆ The rewards

21.1 LEARNING TOOLS ARE CROSS-CULTURAL

The development of Learning Tools is common to all children cross-culturally. Functional Learning programmes to facilitate the early Learning Tools have helped children from many different cultural backgrounds. Because much of the early work is done with a minimum of language, there are few problems in helping children with different language backgrounds. The learning materials are, for the most part, everyday objects and sets of custom-made cards and worksheets, and they can readily be adapted by those working in other countries so that they are culturally appropriate.

21.2 HANOVER, GERMANY – SPECIAL EDUCATION UNIT

In the late 1970s, a day centre for autistic children in Hanover, Germany, became interested in introducing a feeding programme and Functional Learning methods, following a talk at the University of Kassel about the work being done at High Wick, described in Chapter 1. There followed an exchange of visits over several years, during which a series

(Continued)

(Continued)

of workshops was set up for the staff of the centre, focusing on the two main areas of the learning environment and mealtimes.

Although the day centre had many more children and a wider age range – from five years to 18 years – there were many similarities between the two units in structure and function, and in the learning, communication and emotional problems of the children. This provided a broad scope for transferring some of the developments at High Wick into this new environment. In particular, changes were made in the way the school classes were organized to incorporate the principles of Functional Learning, outlined in 3.2, and Functional Learning activities were successfully carried out with some children on an individual basis. Mealtimes, which had been noisy and fraught, were changed dramatically by reducing the amount of food on the table, giving the children small portions and providing individual help where needed, making mealtimes a quieter, more focused experience for the children.

The teacher in charge of the day centre at the time has recently said that Functional Learning contributed to a continuing process of integration of physical, cognitive and emotional aspects of therapeutic intervention which had not happened before. This positive experience has continued and has carried over to the treatment of autistic children as out-patients (Ilse Dittrich, 2007).

21.3 NICOSIA, CYPRUS – INDIVIDUAL FUNCTIONAL LEARNING PROGRAMMES

Nico – 7 years old

Nico, a 7-year-old from Nicosia, Cyprus, was taken to London by his parents for paediatric and psychological assessment. He was found to have minimal neurological dysfunction with poor motor coordination, and his language and learning were delayed. He was referred for Functional Learning and it became clear that he would also need emotional support. His experience of frustration and failure during his early development, because of his poor motor control, resulted in defensive behaviour which interfered with his learning. At times he would become quite passive, using minimal effort, or he would become angry and uncommunicative, refusing to do anything.

An initial intensive programme of Functional Learning sessions three times a week was carried out while the family remained in London. Although Nico had begun to develop some of his Learning Tools, they were not well established, and he still needed a great deal of practice with Placing activities to help his motor coordination. In addition to the learning work with Nico, his parents were given ideas about the simple language they could use to help him begin to understand his difficulties. A video was made of the Functional Learning sessions so that, when the family returned to Cyprus, Nico's parents could continue with the daily programme at home. They were able to video some of their home sessions, and this material was used to help them develop and progress with the Functional Learning activities.

Two visits to see Nico and his family in Nicosia focused on integrating Functional Learning in home and school settings. The family began to understand how they could help him use his emerging Learning Tools in daily activities at home (for more on this, see the individual Learning Tools, in Section II). Nico's teachers were supported in helping him, so that the daily school activities could be adapted to meet his special learning needs and he could integrate in this large mainstream school. Contact was maintained with Nico and his family for a number of years, until he left school and eventually joined the family business.

Andreas – 4 years old

The parents of 4-year-old Andreas wanted their son to be assessed with a view to starting a Functional Learning programme. He had mild cerebral palsy and a local physiotherapist was working with him. Although he had developed some of his Learning Tools his difficult behaviour often interfered with his learning. His language and communication skills were age-appropriate, but he often resorted to immature body language, screaming, pushing and throwing. His noisy, demanding and inflexible behaviour was bewildering to his parents, who either punished him or indulged him. They found it difficult to admit they had a child with special needs, keeping him at home and not letting him mix with other children.

Once they were introduced to Functional Learning and began working with their son, they understood that he had a normal potential, they were able to tell other people about it, and they were proud to show others what their son could do. They organized a work space for Andreas in his bedroom, and began daily Functional Learning sessions, with each of the parents taking turns to work with him. Once Andreas began to settle, becoming quieter and more focused on the learning activities and showing pleasure in what he did, his difficult behaviour began to fall away. He was able to attend a nursery while continuing with the daily Functional Learning programme. By the time he was ready for school at age six, his learning, communication and behaviour were appropriate and he was able to attend a mainstream school, walking into school unaided. Encouraged by Andreas' success, the nursery he attended set aside a work space to provide Functional Learning activities to help other children with developmental delay.

21.4 SLOVENIA – FUNCTIONAL LEARNING TRAINING PROGRAMMES

After attending an International Speech Therapy Conference in Manchester in 1996, where the video *Learning and Communication* was shown, a speech therapist from Ljubljana thought that Functional Learning would benefit the children with developmental delay in her clinic. Since then there has been a continuing association with Katrin Stroh, joined in 2005 by Alan Proctor. Many other practitioners have become involved,

(Continued)

(Continued)

including speech therapists, special teachers, physiotherapists, occupational therapists and psychologists, and so have parents, with interest eventually spreading to Croatia and Montenegro. Visits to Slovenia to run training workshops have been supplemented with distance learning by video, email and telephone consultation. A number of practitioners from Slovenia have been able to make personal visits to London to further their training and experience. Functional Learning programmes have been developed for individual children, and incorporated into a variety of different educational and therapeutic environments.

Four of the original practitioners involved, now trainers themselves, have said that Functional Learning has given them and their colleagues clear strategies for working with children with developmental difficulties, while allowing flexibility and creativity. They have become more confident in knowing how to help the children, by providing an appropriate learning environment and choosing activities suited to their level of development. They report how a mother of a child with severe cerebral palsy, who she described as being 'trapped in his body', said she believed that Functional Learning had provided the 'key' to her son's successful development. He had made slow but steady progress: 'I cannot describe the feelings that a parent of a special needs child feels when their ... child begins to independently use problem-solving skills in their everyday life' (Ana Filipic Dolnicar, Barbara Somen, Slavica Lencek and Mihaela Nena Vovk, 2006).

21.5 A FUNCTIONAL LEARNING WORKSHOP PROGRAMME

Anyone involved in training will have their own training methods. This workshop format has evolved with experience over time. It can be used as a possible model for introducing Functional Learning, and can be adapted to suit different needs and circumstances.

WORKSHOP CONTENT

A three-day workshop programme is suggested to introduce Functional Learning, providing some theoretical background and a good deal of practical experience. This book has been designed as a working manual, and can be referred to as a source of information when running workshops. The examples of learning materials and the video *Learning and Communication*, included on the accompanying CD, can also be used as a training resource.

The main areas to be covered in introductory workshops are:

- observation and development of typical infant play

- introduction to Learning Tools

- play and learning of children with developmental delay

- understanding secondary defensive behaviours

- learning materials and setting up a Functional Learning session

- non-social learning sessions

- activities to facilitate the Learning Tools

- growth of understanding and communication

- problem solving

- feeding, sleeping, and emotional changes in family life

- synchronizing the needs of the child and the parents

- integrating the use of Learning Tools into daily living

- supporting the child in nursery and school.

Guidelines for a three-day workshop programme

DAY 1

Session 1

Introductory session (1.5 hours)

Viewing and discussion of video *Learning and Communication* (1.5 hours)

Session 2

Introduction to Learning Tools for Placing and Banging (1.5 hours)

How to set up Functional Learning sessions

Continue with practical activities to include Learning Tools for Banging and Pairing

(2 hours)

DAY 2

Two sessions

Some ideas for areas to be covered, depending on the needs of participants:

- building on the practical work of Day 1

- communicating with and supporting parents; balancing the needs of the child and those of the parents

- the challenging behaviour of the children

- controversial issues, for example non-social learning sessions

- feeding, toileting and sleeping

- additional activities to extend Learning Tools for Pairing, Matching, Sorting and Sequencing

- daily home practice and learning for living.

(Continued)

> *(Continued)*
>
> *DAY 3*
>
> *One session*
>
> The final day can be flexible and open-ended, allowing for questions and discussion. The following are possible areas of focus:
>
> - reviewing facilitation of the Learning Tools
> - viewing the video again in the light of the experience of the previous two days (1.5 hours)
> - demonstration of a Functional Learning session as a continuous process, using all the Learning Tools discussed so far (1.5 hours).

SOME PRACTICAL SUGGESTIONS

MATERIALS

It can be useful to send potential workshop participants a list of materials to collect beforehand and bring to the workshop. As large wooden bricks are used for many of the early learning activities, it is particularly useful if these can be provided. Other materials can be collected in the home and outside environment. Examples of these materials are given under the individual Learning Tools in Section II and many are illustrated on the CD.

INTRODUCTORY SESSION

One possible way of opening the workshop is for participants and the workshop facilitator to introduce themselves and their work, if appropriate, during the first session and state why they were interested in attending the workshop. If they already have some ideas about Functional Learning, these can also be shared.

SHOWING THE VIDEO

The first part of the 15-minute video *Learning and Communication* follows the development of the play and learning of a little girl for her first two years. This is the foundation and theoretical basis for Functional Learning. After viewing, participants can be asked to write down their observations and share these with the group. One of the things that usually emerges from this first discussion is the importance of play – that play is cross-cultural and that children learn through their play activities, out of which come their early Learning Tools.

The video continues with clips of nine children with developmental delay, all with different diagnoses. This can serve as a stimulus for discussion of the children that participants know of or are working with. It highlights the knowledge and the problems that participants have in common.

The final part of the video shows short longitudinal studies of working sessions with three of the children. This can introduce the practical work of the learning activities with participants working in pairs. With one person acting as the child and the other as the adult, they can start with the large bricks, which are used to facilitate the Learning Tool for picking up and placing. The ensuing discussion allows participants to explore the working environment and the materials used. One important area of focus is the emotional challenges that arise from the child's behaviour. Often, participants demonstrate the behaviour of their most challenging child while they are taking the part of the child. This gives the opportunity for further discussion of strategies to help settle the child – by reducing the amount of material, returning to an earlier familiar activity, slowing down the pace of the activity, or possibly using some therapeutic language.

EXTENDED WORKSHOP PROGRAMME

It may not always be possible to run more than a three-day workshop programme. But for those who are able to commit themselves to a longer training programme, a series of three weekend workshops over a nine-month period can provide more in-depth coverage of Functional Learning as a therapeutic tool. This could include more extensive theoretical information; for the practical work, an increased range of activities to facilitate all the Learning Tools; more examples of how to integrate the Learning Tools into daily life; more on working with parents; therapeutic feeding; and supporting a child in nursery and school.

21.6 THE REWARDS

The rewards for those using the Functional Learning approach are different from those associated with other intervention programmes. They come from seeing the immediacy of response from the child as well as positive changes over time. Close observation while working allows the adult to make subtle changes in the materials or presentation of the activities, without disturbing the child. There is no clapping of hands or social smiles from the child, but instead a growing ability to play and learn, to relate and communicate appropriately.

References

Baratta-Lorton, Mary (ed.) (1998) *Mathematics Their Way: An Activity-centred Mathematics Programme for Early Childhood.* New edn. Boston: Addison Wesley Longman.

Bee, Helen and Boyd, Denise (2004) *The Developing Child.* 10th edn. Boston: Allyn and Bacon.

Bellman, M.H. (2001) Commentary on Patrick Bolton, 'Developmental assessment', *Advances in Psychiatric Treatment*, 7: 40–2.

Bloom, Lois (1993) *The Transition from Infancy to Language: Acquiring the Power of Expression.* Cambridge: Cambridge University Press.

Brooks, Richard (no date) 'A description of an asocial lesson', in Waldon approach to education. Online at: http://www.waldonassociation.org.uk (accessed 19 May 2007).

Bruce, Tina (2001) *Learning Through Play: Babies, Toddlers and the Foundation Years.* London: Hodder and Stoughton.

Carroll, Roz (2003) '"At the boundary between chaos and order": what psychotherapy and neuroscience have in common', in Jenny Corrigall and Heward Wilkinson (eds), *Revolutionary Connections: Psychotherapy and Neuroscience.* London: Karnac. pp. 191–213.

Czerniewska, Pam (1992) *Learning About Writing.* Oxford: Blackwell.

Damasio, Antonio R. (1998) 'Emotion in the perspective of an integrated nervous system', *Brain Research Reviews*, 26: 83–6.

Department for Children, Schools and Families (2002) 'Birth to Three Matters: A Framework to Support Children in Their Earliest Years'. Online at: http://www.standards.dfes.gov.uk/primary/publications/foundation_stage/9 40463/ (accessed 14 September 2007).

Department for Education and Skills (2005) 'Excellence and Enjoyment: Social and Emotional Aspects of Learning Guidance'. Online at: http://www.standards.dfes. gov.uk/primary/publications/banda/seal/ (accessed 16 September 2007).

Department for Education and Skills (2007) 'Practice Guidance for the Early Years Foundation Stage'. Online at: http://www.standards/dfes.gov.uk/ primary/publications/foundation_stage/eyfs/ (accessed 15 September 2007).

Dittrich, Ilse (2007) Personal communication.

Filipic Dolnicar, Ana, Somen, Barbara, Lencek, Slavica and Nena Vovk, Mihaela (2006) Personal communication.

Forbes, Ruth (2004) *Beginning to Play: Young Children from Birth to Three.* Maidenhead: Open University Press.

Freud, Sigmund (1925) *The Standard Edition of the Complete Psychological Works of Sigmund Freud, Vol XIX (1923–1925): The Ego and the Id and Other Works.* Transl. by James Strachey (ed.), 2001. London: Vintage. pp. 233–40.

Gerhardt, Sue (2004) *Why Love Matters: How Affection Shapes a Baby's Brain.* Hove: Brunner-Routledge.

Giedd, Jay (2002) 'Inside the teenage brain', interview with neuroscientist Jay Giedd. Online at: http://www.pbs.org/wgbh/pages/frontline/shows/teenbrain/interviews/giedd.html (accessed 3 September 2007).

Goldblatt, Max (1964) 'Report on lectures to staff at High Wick Hospital'. Unpublished report.

Goldschmied, Elinor and Jackson, Sonia (2003) *People Under Three: Young Children in Day Care.* 2nd edn. Oxford: Routledge.

Greenspan, Stanley and Wieder, Serena with Robin Simons (1998) *The Child with Special Needs: Encouraging Intellectual and Emotional Growth.* Da Capo Press (US).

Greenspan, Stanley and Wieder, Serena (2006) *Infant and Early Childhood Mental Health: A Comprehensive Developmental Approach to Assessment and Intervention.* Washington, DC: American Psychiatric Publishing.

Hughes, Anita M. (2006) *Developing Play for the Under Threes: The Treasure Basket and Heuristic Play.* London: David Fulton.

Jernberg, Ann M. and Booth, Phyllis B. (1999) *Theraplay: Helping Parents and Children Build Better Relationships Through Attachment-Based Play.* 2nd edn. San Francisco: Jossey-Bass.

Kanner, Leo (1973) *Childhood Psychosis: Initial Studies and New Insights.* Washington, DC: V.H. Winston.

Koman, Aleta and Myers, Edward (2000) *The Parenting Survival Kit: How to Make it Through the Parenting Years with Your Family, Sanity and Wallet Intact.* New York: Berkley Publishing.

Kraemer, S. (1987) 'Working with parents: casework or psychotherapy', *Journal of Child Psychology and Psychiatry*, 28: 207–13.

Lillard, Angeline Stoll (2007) *Montessori: The Science Behind the Genius.* New York: Oxford University Press.

Lindon, Jennie (2001) *Understanding Children's Play.* Cheltenham: Nelson Thornes.

Meisels, Samuel J. and Atkins-Burnett, Sally (2000) 'The elements of early childhood assessment', in Jack P. Shonkoff and Samuel J. Meisels (eds), *Handbook of Early Childhood Intervention*, 2nd edn. Cambridge: Cambridge University Press.

Moyles, Janet R. (ed.) (2005) *The Excellence of Play.* 2nd edn. Maidenhead: Open University Press.

Osofsky, Joy D. and Thompson, M. Dewana (2000) 'Adaptive and maladaptive parenting: perspectives on risk and protective factors', in Jack P. Shonkoff and Samuel J. Meisels (eds), *Handbook of Early Childhood Intervention*, 2nd edn. Cambridge: Cambridge University Press.

Phillips, Adam (1988) *Winnicott.* London: Fontana Press.

Pruett, Kyle D. (1998) 'Role of the father', *Pediatrics*, 102(5): 1253–61.

Qualifications and Curriculum Authority (2000) 'Curriculum Guidance for the Foundation Stage'. Online at: http://www.standards.dfes.gov.uk/primary/publications/foundation_stage/63593/ (accessed 14 September 2007).

Robson, Sue (2006) *Developing Thinking and Understanding in Young Children.* Abingdon: Routledge.

Salo, Frances Thomson (2005) *You and Your Baby.* London: Karnac.

Schore, Allan (2001) 'The American Bowlby', interview by Roz Carroll. Online at: http://www.thinkbody.co.uk/papers/interview-with-allan-s.html (accessed 14 August 2007).

Siegel, Daniel J. (1999) *The Developing Mind: How Relationships and the Brain Interact to Shape Who We Are*. New York: Guilford Press.

Stern, Daniel N. (1985) *The Interpersonal World of the Infant: A View from Psychoanalysis and Developmental Psychology*. New York: Basic Books.

Stroh, Katrin (1986) 'Introduction', in *The Impossible Made Possible...: The Collected Papers of George Stroh*, published by the Trustees of the George Stroh Memorial Fund.

Stroh, George and Buick, David (1970) 'The effect of relative sensory isolation on the behaviour of two autistic children', in *The Impossible Made Possible...: The Collected Papers of George Stroh*, published by the Trustees of the George Stroh Memorial Fund, 1986.

Stroh, Katrin and Robinson, Thelma (1988) 'Observations and speculations on the emotional responses of the aphasic child', *Child Language Teaching and Therapy*, 4(1): 60–71.

Stroh, Katrin and Robinson, Thelma (1991) 'Developmental delay in young children: redressing the balance for child and parents', *Child Language Teaching and Therapy*, 7(1): 1–26.

Stroh, Katrin, Robinson, Thelma and Stroh, George (1986) 'A therapeutic feeding programme. I: Theory and practice of feeding'. *Developmental Medicine and Child Neurology*, 28: 3–10.

The Concise Oxford Dictionary of Current English (1995). 9th edn. Oxford: Oxford University Press.

Thomas, Ruth (1964) 'Services for High Wick Hospital for mentally disturbed children'. Unpublished report.

Thompson, G. Brian, Tunmer, William E. and Nicholson, Tom (eds) (1993) *Reading Acquisition Processes*. Clevedon: Multilingual Matters.

Trevarthen, C. and Aitken, K.J. (1994) 'Brain development, infant communication and empathy disorders: intrinsic factors in child mental health', *Development and Psychopathology*, 6: 599–635.

Waldon, Geoffrey (1966) 'The Education of Retarded and Handicapped Children'. Unpublished paper. (Reprinted 1982.)

Waldon, Geoffrey (1980) 'Understanding understanding: an introduction to a personal view of the educational needs of children', revised 1985. Online at: http://www.waldonassociation.org.uk/understanding%20understanding.htm (accessed 14 September 2007).

Waldon, Geoffrey (1981) *Understanding Understanding*. Video available from Concord Media at www.concordvideo.co.uk

Waldon, Geoffrey (1985) 'The Process of Sorting and Matching as Mental Operations Generating New Experience in Child Development'. Unpublished paper.

Waldon, Geoffrey (1988) Personal communication.

Whitebread, David (ed.) (1996) *Teaching and Learning in the Early Years*. London: Routledge.

Williamson, G. Gordon and Anzalone, Marie E. (2001) *Sensory Integration and Self-Regulation in Infants and Toddlers: Helping Very Young Children Interact With Their Environment*. Washington, DC: Zero to Three.

Winstock, April (2005) *Eating and Drinking Difficulties in Children: A Guide for Practitioners*. Brackley: Speechmark.

Index

Added to a page number 'g' denotes glossary and 'f' denotes a figure

AUTISM AND UNDERSTANDING

The Waldon Approach to Child Development

Walter Solomon with **Chris Holland** and **Mary Jo Middleton**

The author sets out an approach based on Dr Geoffrey Waldon's philosophy of the development of understanding, which centres on helping children learn-how-to-learn.

The book includes:

- The inspirational and well documented story of the author's son, diagnosed at two with autism and as 'basically sub-normal', now a successful professional with a wife and child.

- An introduction to Geoffrey Waldon's theory and working methods.

- Testimony from parents and teachers, covering autism and a range of learning difficulties.

This book does not offer a 'miracle cure' for autism, although the author aims to counteract the prevailing view that autism is a lifetime condition. The author demonstrates that with the appropriate intervention, children with autism - and other special needs - can gain a fuller understanding of the world and learn to take a constructive and contributing place in it.

CONTENTS

Early Days 1968-1972 \ School Years 1972-1987 \ College Years, UK and Israel 1987-1998 \ Work and Marriage 1998-2011 \ The Waldon Theory of Child Development and the Waldon Approach \ Centres Influenced by Geoffrey Waldon \ Case Studies of Children on the Autistic Spectrum \ Not Only for Autism - More Case Studies \ Functional Reading: A Special Orientation of the Approach

READERSHIP

Teachers, therapists, doctors, parents and special interest groups

2012 • 240 pages

 Cloth (978-1-4462-0923-3) • £70.00
Paper (978-1-4462-0924-0) • £23.99

ALSO FROM SAGE